History of Africa for Kids

A Captivating Guide to African History, from Ancient Times through the Middle Ages to the Modern Era

© Copyright 2022

All Rights Reserved. No part of this book may be reproduced in any form without permission in writing from the author. Reviewers may quote brief passages in reviews.

Disclaimer

No part of this publication may be reproduced or transmitted in any form or by any means, mechanical or electronic, including photocopying or recording, or by any information storage and retrieval system, or transmitted by email without permission in writing from the publisher.

While all attempts have been made to verify the information provided in this publication, neither the author nor the publisher assumes any responsibility for errors, omissions or contrary interpretations of the subject matter herein.

This book is for entertainment purposes only. The views expressed are those of the author alone, and should not be taken as expert instruction or commands. The reader is responsible for his or her own actions.

Adherence to all applicable laws and regulations, including international, federal, state and local laws governing professional licensing, business practices, advertising and all other aspects of doing business in the US, Canada, UK or any other jurisdiction is the sole responsibility of the purchaser or reader.

Neither the author nor the publisher assumes any responsibility or liability whatsoever on the behalf of the purchaser or reader of these materials. Any perceived slight of any individual or organization is purely unintentional.

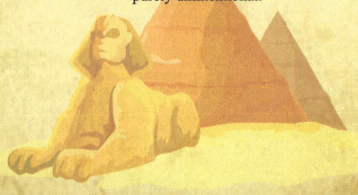

Table of Contents

Part 1: African History for Kids — 1

Introduction — 2

Chapter 1: Ancient Africa — 3

Chapter 2: The Kingdom of Egypt — 5

Chapter 3: The Kingdom of Kush — 14

Chapter 4: The Kingdom of Aksum — 21

Chapter 5: Medieval Africa — 31

Chapter 6: The Ghana Empire — 42

Chapter 7: The Kanem-Bornu Empire — 49

Chapter 8: The Mali Empire — 57

Chapter 9: Colonization and Enslavement — 65

Chapter 10: Decolonization and Independence — 75

Part 2: Ancient Africa for Kids — 82

Chapter 1: The Kingdom of Kerma — 84

Chapter 2: The Egyptian Kingdom — 91

Chapter 3: The Kingdom of Kush — 99

Chapter 4: Ancient Carthage — 106

Chapter 5: Roman North Africa/Africa Proconsularis — 113

Chapter 6: The Kingdom of Aksum — 120

Chapter 7: The Empire of Ancient Ghana — 127

Chapter 8: Society and Famous Rulers — 133

Chapter 9: Culture and Art	142
Chapter 10: Myths and Religion	149
Part 3: Medieval African for Kids	**155**
Introduction	156
Chapter 1: The African Middle Ages	157
Chapter 2: The Ghana Empire	165
Chapter 3: The Kanem-Bornu Empire	172
Chapter 4: The Kingdom of Benin	179
Chapter 5: The Mali Empire	186
Chapter 6: Emperor Mansa Musa	194
Chapter 7: The Kingdom of Abyssiania	201
Chapter 8: The Songhay Kingdom	208
Chapter 9: Society and Famous Rulers	214
Chapter 10: Culture and Art	221
Answer Key	228
If you want to learn more about tons of other exciting historical periods, check out our other books!	232
Bibliography	233

Part 1:

AFRICAN HISTORY FOR KIDS

A CAPTIVATING GUIDE TO THE HISTORY OF AFRICA

CAPTIVATING HISTORY

INTRODUCTION

Africa is the second-largest continent on earth. It makes up 20 percent of the earth's landmass, which means there are many countries in Africa that all have their own rich histories to be unearthed! So, put your exploring cap on, and get ready to learn all about the history of this fascinating continent and its people.

Fun Fact: Africa is more than three times the size of the United States!

Throughout this book, you will explore the many kingdoms and empires of Africa from ancient times to today. Travel through the ancient Egyptian, Kush, and Aksum kingdoms before reaching medieval Africa. Then, be awed by the impressive Ghana, Kanem-Bornu, and Mali empires. You will discover the shocking truth about the horrific transatlantic slave trade and the colonization (settling with and controlling the indigenous/native peoples of an area) of Africa before finally learning how it all came to an end and how African countries regained their independence, which allows a (country to govern and control itself.

Watch history come alive with interesting images, fun facts, and amazing activities!

Chapter 1: Ancient Africa

Millions of years ago, Africa became the birthplace of human life. Many firsts for humanity took place on this continent. All the people of today are part of the species known as *Homo sapiens*, but before this, there were many other (now extinct) species of humans. One of the earliest types of humans was *Homo habilis*, who lived around 2.5 million years ago in the eastern and southern areas of Africa. *Homo habilis* were the first humans to use tools.

The discovery and ability to use fire was a vital step in the evolution of mankind. This was also made by early Africans approximately 1.4 million years ago.

Fun Fact: *Homo* is the Latin word for man.

The final step between the extinct *Homo erectus* species and modern-day *Homo sapiens* is also believed to have happened in Africa since the oldest fossils of modern man were found in Ethiopia.

Fun Fact: Africa is home to the oldest known examples of fishing, jewelry, math, animal domestication, crop cultivation, and more.

Seeing as it was the starting point for human life, it is perhaps no surprise that Africa was also home to one of the oldest human civilizations: Ancient Egypt. Ancient Egypt is estimated to have begun around 3150 BCE and ended in 30 BCE. It was centered around the Nile River on the northeastern coast of Africa. Before ancient Egypt began to flourish, there were only two other known homes to human civilizations: the Indus Valley (modern Afghanistan, Pakistan, and

India) from 3300 BCE to 1900 BCE and the Mesopotamian civilizations (modern Iraq, Syria, and Turkey) from 3500 BCE to 500 BCE.

Many empires and kingdoms would follow ancient Egypt. Just below ancient Egypt, the Kingdom of Kush was established in 1070 BCE. Later, the neighboring Kingdom of Aksum would flourish. It was followed by the Ghana Empire, the Kanem-Bornu Empire, and the Mali Empire.

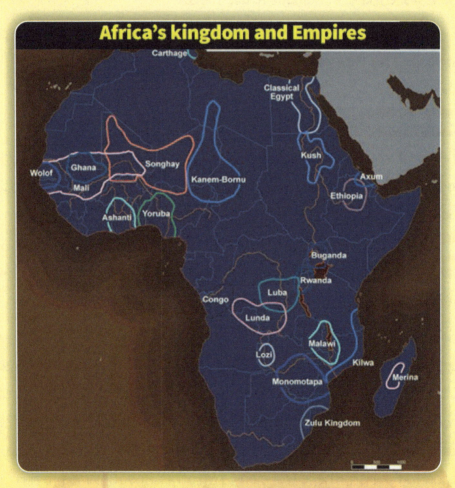

Map of the kingdoms of ancient Africa

Chapter 2: The Kingdom of Egypt

In this chapter, we're going to discover a little more information about the Kingdom of Egypt. We could fill a whole book on ancient Egypt (and we have – check out our *Ancient Egypt for Kids* book to learn more), but for now, we will just cover the main highlights of this important time in early African history.

The start of the ancient Egyptian civilization is known as the *Early Dynastic Period*. It was the start of Egypt being ruled by dynasties. A *dynasty* is a ruling family that passes leadership down through the family line.

Fun Fact: During the three thousand years of ancient Egypt, there were thirty different dynasties!

The first king of the Early Dynastic Period was *King Menes*. He was responsible for uniting Upper and Lower Egypt into one civilization and building the famous white-walled city of *Memphis*, which became the capital of ancient Egypt.

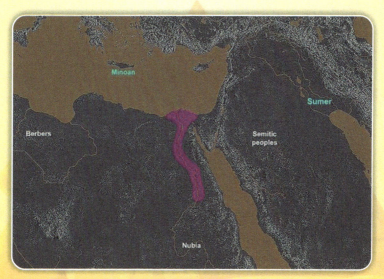

Map of the Early Dynastic Period of Egypt

Egypt is located in the northeast of Africa toward the top of the Nile River around the Nile Delta, where the river joins the Mediterranean Sea. One of the main reasons that the ancient Egyptian civilization was able to thrive was its access to the Nile River.

Fun Fact: The Nile is the longest river in the world, flowing 4,132 miles northward toward the Mediterranean Sea.

The Nile was not only a great source of drinking water. It was also vitally important for growing crops. Once a year, the river would flood, bringing in *silt*, a fine soil useful for planting and growing seeds. Without this yearly flooding, droughts could occur, causing widespread *famine* and starvation.

The unusual northward direction that the Nile flowed in was part of its success. Goods and building materials could be transported from the south. It was thanks to the Nile that the ancient Egyptians were able to build their impressive pyramids and monuments.

The first thing that likely comes to mind when thinking of Egypt is the pyramids. However, the first pyramids weren't built until five or six hundred years after the ancient Egyptian civilization began in the period known as the *Old Kingdom*. The most famous pyramid of all, *the Great Pyramid of Giza*, was built during this time by *King Khufu*.

Fun Fact: The Great Pyramid of Giza is one of the Seven Wonders of the Ancient World and can still be visited today!

The Great Pyramid was the first and largest pyramid (481 feet high) in the burial complex of Giza. The huge structure is made of 2.3 million stone blocks that weigh between 2.5 to 15 tons each! Historians are still unsure exactly how the Great Pyramid was built, but they estimate that between 20,000 to 100,000 people could have been involved!

Fun Fact: The Great Pyramid was built in just 23 years, meaning that 100,000 blocks a year, 285 blocks a day, or 1 block every 2 minutes had to be located, moved, prepared, and put in place! Phew, that sounds like a lot of work!

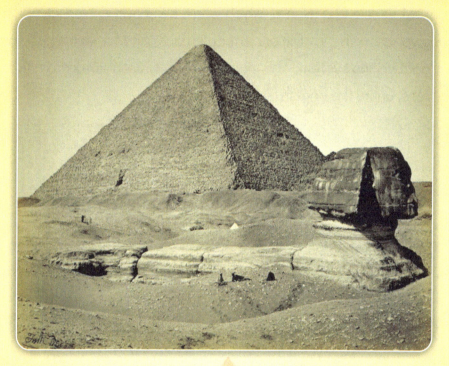

The Great Pyramid of Giza and the Sphinx (https://flic.kr/p/5JR1Dz)

Fun Fact: For almost 4,400 years, until the Eiffel Tower was built in 1889 in Paris, the Great Pyramid was the tallest structure on earth built by hand!

As well as building pyramids on the burial grounds, other monuments would also be built, such as *the Great Sphinx* in the Giza complex. A sphinx is a mythical creature with the head of a man and the body of a lion. The Great Sphinx was carved out of a single piece of limestone. It is an impressive 66-foot high and 240-foot-long construction, making it one of the biggest statues in the world!

Fun Fact: It is believed that King Khufu included the Great Sphinx in his burial complex to watch over the dead.

In the burial complexes, there would also be grave markings known as *steles*. These large stone tablets would contain information about important people and events, which would be shown in *hieroglyphics*. Hieroglyphics was what the ancient Egyptians used for writing. It was a *pictorial* writing system. This means that they used pictures instead of letters, unlike the English alphabet.

Egyptian stele (https://flic.kr/p/XstBqa)

The most famous example of a stele ever discovered is the *Rosetta Stone*. The Rosetta Stone was accidentally discovered in 1799 CE by soldiers in Napoleon Bonaparte's army who were digging battle foundations near the Nile Delta. The Rosetta Stone was an incredibly important discovery. It helped historians finally *decipher* (understand and translate) Egyptian hieroglyphics. Since the language was no longer used, they could not read the hieroglyphics. However, the Rosetta Stone was written in three different languages, including hieroglyphics, so they could translate it based on the ancient Greek writing that was also on the stone.

Another type of structure still standing from ancient Egypt is the temples that were built to worship their many gods. These temples would be just as impressive as the pyramids. They often contained massive statues of pharaohs and gods, as well as huge stone columns.

An example of an Egyptian column
(https://flic.kr/p/XpJRPQ)

The ancient Egyptians built their impressive pyramids for a few reasons. First and foremost, they were used as burial grounds. But, of course, pyramids didn't need to be so large just to bury the dead. These huge monuments were created primarily due to their religious beliefs. They believed that to go on living in the afterlife, your name needed to be remembered by the living. Considering we are still talking about ancient Egypt and its kings, it's safe to say they achieved their goal of being remembered!

As well as King Menes and King Khufu, there were many other famous ancient Egyptian kings and pharaohs (pharaoh is another name for king and began to be used during the New Kingdom Period). Interestingly, one of the most famous pharaohs of all is also the most unlikely.

King Tutankhamun only ruled for ten years. He took the throne when he was only nine years old. When he died at the age of nineteen, he didn't leave behind a great monument to be remembered by. However, he became one of the most famous kings precisely because of his obscurity.

The tomb of King Tutankhamun was discovered in 1922 CE by *Howard Carter*, a British archaeologist. Many of the other bigger tombs in *the Valley of the Kings* were raided and their objects stolen years before modern historians found them. But because it was the smallest in the complex and the most hidden, King Tut's tomb remained undisturbed for over 3,200 years!

Fun Fact: Despite the tomb being the smallest in the Valley of the Kings, it still contained around five thousand artifacts! In fact, it took historians seventeen years to *catalog* (record) everything inside!

Among the artifacts in the tomb, the mummy of King Tutankhamun was also still there. It was perfectly preserved. Perhaps the most well-known artifact found inside the tomb was the blue and gold mask of the pharaoh.

Mask of Tutankhamun
https://commons.wikimedia.org/wiki/File:Tutmask.jpg

Fun Fact: King Tutankhamun's mother-in-law, *Nefertiti*, is also very famous due to a well-preserved bust of her face that was discovered.

While King Tut didn't gain notoriety until thousands of years after his death, another very famous pharaoh of ancient Egypt, *Rameses II* (or Rameses the Great), is best remembered due to the enormous number of monuments built in his name. In fact, there is virtually no monument in Egypt that doesn't mention him!

Fun Fact: Rameses II lived to be 96 years old. He ruled for so long that many of his subjects had never known another pharaoh, and they feared that when he died, the world would end!

Two other famous pharaohs often aren't thought of as being Egyptian rulers due to their Greek heritage. *Alexander the Great* conquered the *Persian Empire*, which had been in control of Egypt. This made him the new pharaoh. While he was in power, he created a new capital city, *Alexandria*. Although this city was Egyptian, it did not adopt only the Egyptian culture. In fact, it was very Greek in nature. It was here that *Cleopatra VII* was born. She was the last pharaoh of Egypt. Cleopatra is remembered for her beauty and her love affair with two powerful Greek rulers, *Julius Caesar* and *Mark Antony*.

If you'd like to learn more about ancient Egypt, including more details on their pharaohs, what life was like, their religious beliefs, and why they mummified the dead, check out our *Ancient Egypt for Kids* guide!

Chapter 2 Activities

1. Who was King Menes? What did he do?
2. Where is Egypt located?
3. Why was the Nile so important?
4. What is a sphinx?
5. Why was the Rosetta Stone important?

Chapter 2 Answers

1. King Menes was the first ruler of ancient Egypt. He united Upper and Lower Egypt and built the capital city of Memphis.

2. Egypt is located in the northeast of Africa toward the top of the Nile River, where the river joins the Mediterranean Sea.

3. The Nile was vital to the Egyptian civilization since it provided drinking water and water for crops. It was also used to transport goods and stone for building cities and monuments.

4. A sphinx is a mythical creature with the head of a man and the body of a lion. Fun

    Fact: Both Greek and Asian mythology adopted the sphinx. Both of these versions had wings.

5. The Rosetta Stone was important since it helped historians finally read hieroglyphics.

Chapter 3: The Kingdom of Kush

Our next ancient African kingdom is the Kingdom of Kush, which is also often referred to as *Nubia*. Nubia was located just below Egypt to the south. The two kingdoms had many ties and similarities. Kush and its capital cities were located around the Nile River, White River, and Blue River. Today, the country of Sudan is where Kush used to be.

Before it gained its independence in 1070 BCE, Kush was part of Egypt. But with the decline of the New Kingdom of Egypt around that time, Kush was able to break free of Egyptian rule and establish its own kingdom. The city-state of *Napata* became its capital.

Fun Fact: Nubia was often nicknamed the "Land of the Bow" because the bow and arrow was their weapon of choice in battle.

Map of ancient Kush, ancient Egypt, and the surrounding areas.

In 746 BCE, the *Kushites* managed to conquer Egypt under the rule of *King Piye*. This began the 25th Dynasty of Egypt. Egypt remained under Kushite control until 653 BCE, when they were driven out by the *Assyrians*.

Fun Fact: The Assyrians and later rulers of Egypt tried to erase the evidence of Kushite rule by destroying many of their statues and steles.

The final era of the Kingdom of Kush is often referred to as the *Meroitic Period*. The Meroitic Period began in 300 BCE and continued until the Kingdom of Kush became part of the *Kingdom of Aksum* in 330 CE. During this time, the capital city of Kush became *Meroë*. Meroë was a port city located on the Nile River. It was useful as a trade route to other areas. Not only was the soil good for crops there, but it was also very close to iron and gold mines. These were the main sources of wealth for the Kingdom of Kush.

There were many similarities between the Kushite and Egyptian cultures. The Kushites believed in the Egyptian gods. They built pyramids and mummified their dead. The Kushite pyramids were smaller than the Egyptian ones. They were no taller than 98 feet high, and their bases were around 22 feet wide. To put that into perspective, the Great Pyramid of Giza is four times taller and has a base of 756 feet! The Kushite pyramids were also far steeper than their Egyptian counterparts, with an incline of seventy degrees compared to the fifty-degree angle of the Egyptian ones.

Fun Fact: Although the Kushite pyramids may have been smaller, there were more pyramids in one burial complex in Meroë than in the whole of Egypt!

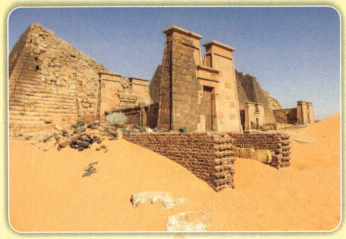

The pyramids of Meroë. Credit: Christopher Michel, Flickr.
(https://flic.kr/p/S55wS4   https://flic.kr/p/QQ4X6B)

Like many ancient civilizations, religion was a very important part of the daily life and culture of Kush. The Kushites adopted many of the Egyptian gods as their own. The main god they worshiped was *Amun*, who was often depicted as a man with the head of a ram or as a ram. Amun was a creator god and the god of the sun and air. Amun was less clearly defined than other gods. His name roughly means "hidden one" or "invisible." Because of this, the people could define him as what they needed him to be.

An important Kushite deity was *Apedemak*, who was the god of war. He had the head of a lion. His wife, *Amesemi*, was a protective goddess who wore a falcon-shaped crown.

Like ancient Egypt, the Kingdom of Kush was based on a class system. At the top were the king and priests. The priests were so powerful that they decided who would become king and when the king died. If they believed the king was no longer a suitable ruler, they would tell him that the god Amun had decided that it was time for him to die.

The classes below the ruler and priests were the artisans and scribes. The artisans were responsible for making items out of gold and iron. These were the two most important goods that Kush exported and used. Iron was used to make strong weapons and tools. Gold provided wealth and would often be traded with their Egyptian neighbors. The next class was made up of the farmers. The large majority of Kushites were farmers, and they mainly grew barley and wheat or cotton to make clothes. Finally, the lowest social class was made up of slaves and servants.

Although the Kushite culture was similar to the Egyptians, they had many differences. After the 1st century BCE, the ruler, *Arkamani*, decided that Kush needed to move away from the Egyptian culture and embrace their own. He ended the priests' power over the throne and encouraged the worship of Kushite gods. He also discarded the Egyptian hieroglyphic writing in favor of a new Kushite language, *Meroitic*.

Fun Fact: To this day, the Meroitic language has still not been deciphered.

Arkamani also introduced queens, known as *Kandakes* or *Candaces*, to Kush. The throne would be passed down *matrilineally*. This means the family would be traced through the female line.

The Kushites also looked different from their Egyptian neighbors. In Egyptian artwork, the Kushites are shown to have darker skin and shorter hair. The Kushites also wore different clothing, favoring patterned material, animal skins, and big earrings.

Artifacts from the Kingdom of Kush
(https://flic.kr/p/Wygoka)

Chapter 3 Activities

1. Where was the Kingdom of Kush located?

2. What other name is sometimes used to describe the Kingdom of Kush?

3. Did the Kushite culture and customs resemble any other culture?

4. What weapon did the Kushite soldiers famously use?

5. What were the main sources of wealth for Kush?

Chapter 3 Answers

1. **The Kingdom of Kush was located to the south of Egypt around the Nile River, White River, and Blue River in what is now the country of Sudan.**

2. **The Kingdom of Kush is also sometimes called Nubia.**

3. **The Kushite culture and customs strongly resembled the Egyptians.**

4. **The Kushite soldiers famously used bows and arrows for weapons.**

5. **Their main sources of wealth were gold and iron.**

Chapter 4: The Kingdom of Aksum

The Kingdom of Aksum, also referred to as *Axum*, was located in East Africa in the area known as the *Horn of Africa* by the Red Sea. As well as covering the northern part of modern-day Ethiopia, it also covered parts of other countries, such as Eritrea, Sudan, Yemen, and Saudi Arabia.

Fun Fact: The city of Axum still exists in Ethiopia today. It is one of the oldest continually occupied cities in Africa.

Map of the Kingdom of Aksum.

According to legend, the Kingdom of Aksum was founded by the son of *King Solomon* and the *Queen of Sheba*. King Solomon was the king of Israel. He appears in the Hebrew Bible, the Christian Old Testament, and the Islamic Quran. King Solomon is depicted as a wise ruler. Perhaps the most well-known story of his wisdom is the one in which two mothers came to him. They both claimed that a baby was theirs. King Solomon tricked the women by saying that the solution was to cut the baby in half. Solomon knew that the real mother would give up her child to the other woman since she would do anything to save it. One of the women agreed to the solution, so he was able to determine who the real mother was and return the baby to her unharmed. It is because of his wisdom that the Queen of Sheba reportedly decided to visit King Solomon.

While King Solomon can be traced back to a real ruler, there is no evidence other than the biblical stories that the Queen of Sheba existed. But, according to legend, she was from the Aksum area. The gifts of gold, spices, and precious gems she brought with her also help support this theory, as these can all be found in the Horn of Africa. It is said that while she was visiting Solomon, the Queen of Sheba fell pregnant with his son, *Menelik*. He was raised as a Jew and eventually founded the *Solomonic Dynasty*. Later, Aksum would go on to embrace Christianity, but many Ethiopian Jews refused to adopt Christianity and still practice Judaism to this day.

King Menelik would eventually go and meet his father, Solomon. It is rumored that the son of a high priest, *Azariah*, went to Aksum with Menelik. He stole the *Ark of the Covenant* and brought it to Aksum with him. King Solomon began to chase after Azariah when he discovered it was missing. However, he had a dream that it needed to be with his son. So, he returned to Jerusalem and commanded his priests to keep its disappearance a secret.

Fun Fact: The Ark of the Covenant is believed to contain the two stone tablets that the Ten Commandments are written on. The sacred object is said to be a wooden box covered in gold with two golden *cherubim* (cherubs or angels) on top called the *mercy seat*.

But let's look at the real facts instead of legends. We know the Kingdom of Aksum didn't become more powerful until around 100 CE. We don't know whether the kingdom was a different one from what Menelik ruled. This is because the early records of Aksum are scarce.

Aksum became powerful because it had control over major points of trade. They were also successful in their farming efforts due to the rich soil and reliable rainy season. Aksum was connected to many trade routes, including the Nile River, the Red Sea, and the Gulf of Aden. The main trade city was *Adulis*. All sorts of desirable objects and necessary items were exchanged here. The Aksum people would trade ivory and gold with India and the Mediterranean. The Romans would trade olive oil or wine. The Indians had spices and jewels to offer. The Aksumites also grew wheat and barley, which they would trade.

Fun Fact: Because of traders coming from all over the world to Aksum, Greek was the most commonly used language by merchants.

While Greek was commonly used, the Aksumites also had their own language, *Ge'ez*. Ge'ez was written in the *boustrophedon* style. This means it was written from left to right. The next line would be from right to left, and it would continue to alternate the direction of each line. The oldest version of the language did not have vowels. However, when Christianity was introduced, vowels were also introduced. This happened because it allowed the people to convert the Bible into Ge'ez more easily.

Coin of the Aksumite King Ezana
(https://commons.wikimedia.org/wiki/File:Endubis.jpg#/media/File:Endubis.jpg)

Because of their strong trading culture, the Aksumites also minted their own coins. These were made from gold, silver, or copper. They were one of the few ancient kingdoms to have done this. Gold coins were usually used for foreign trade. They would be inscribed with Greek. The silver and copper coins would have Ge'ez on them. The first Aksumite coins were similar in design and weight to the Roman ones. They depicted the ruling king, *King Endubis*, religious symbols of the sun and moon, and a type of wheat called *teff*.

When *King Ezana* was in power, he decided to change the symbols on the coins to contain a cross. This demonstrates the religious change to Christianity that had taken place. King Ezana is thought to have become king sometime between 320 and 325. It is rumored that he converted to Christianity because of a former slave and tutor of his, *Frumentius*.

Aksum became the first Christian state in Africa, and it was one of the first states in the world to make it the state religion. Ezana may have been influenced to convert due to a desire to strengthen trade deals with the Romans. A stele called the *Ezana Stone* depicts King Ezana's conversion and conquest of nearby areas, such as Meroë. The Ezana Stone has been compared to the Rosetta Stone because it is also written in three different languages. The three languages on the Ezana Stone are Ge'ez, Greek, and *Sabaean*.

The Ezana Stone. Credit: Wikimedia Commons, Sailko
(https://commons.wikimedia.org/wiki/File:Aksum,_iscrizione_di_re_ezana,_in_greco,_sabeo_e_ge%27ez,_330-350_dc_ca._10.jpg#/media/File:Aksum,_iscrizione_di_re_ezana,_in_greco,_sabeo_e_ge'ez,_330-350_dc_ca._10.jpg)

Close-up of the Ezana Stone. Credit: Wikimedia Commons, Sailko
(https://commons.wikimedia.org/wiki/File:Aksum,_iscrizione_di_re_ezana,_in_greco,_sabeo_e_ge%27ez,_330-350_dc_ca._14.jpg#/media/File:Aksum,_iscrizione_di_re_ezana,_in_greco,_sabeo_e_ge'ez,_330-350_dc_ca._14.jpg)

The Ezana Stone and many other steles were found in the town of Aksum near the Church of Our Lady Mary of Zion. This is where the Ark of the Covenant is rumored to be hidden. The steles are sometimes referred to as *obelisks*. These are tall stone monuments that are *monolithic*. This means they were carved from a single piece of stone. One of the steles here, known as the Great Stele (also spelled as Great Stela), is likely to have been the biggest monolith ever attempted. However, because of its massive 520-ton weight, it fell during construction.

The Obelisk of Aksum weighs less than half of the Great Stele. It is about 160 tons and is almost 80 feet tall. Just like its bigger counterpart, the Obelisk of Aksum also fell at some point. In 1937, invading Italian soldiers removed the obelisk, and it was taken back to Rome, where it was re-erected. They had to cut the obelisk into three since it was so big! Despite a United Nations ruling in 1947 that said it should be returned to Ethiopia, the stele remained in Rome for seventy years. It was returned in 2005.

Fun Fact: In 2008, 1,700 years after it was first built, the monument was once again erected in the same place.

The third-largest stele was built to honor King Ezana. It is the largest unbroken stele left standing. It is thought to be the last one built, as the shift to Christianity meant that steles were no longer used as burial markers.

The Obelisk of Aksum
(https://commons.wikimedia.org/wiki/File:Salt_and_Havell_(1809)
_The_Obelisk_at_Axum.png#/media/File:Salt_and_Havell_(1809)_The_Obelisk_at_Axum.png)

The Kingdom of Aksum reached its peak during King Ezana's rule. It thrived until 960. According to legend, it was conquered by a foreign queen. However, many factors led to the ultimate downfall of the Kingdom of Aksum. Perhaps most crucially was the loss of its trade routes during wars against the Islamic armies. The once fertile soil they used for crops also began to dry out, and the *Justinian Plague* killed many of the Aksum people.

Fun Fact: The Justinian Plague was the first known occurrence of the bubonic plague. It may have been responsible for as many as fifty million deaths!

Chapter 4 Activities

1. What is another common name for the Kingdom of Aksum?

    A) Egypt B) Axum C) Kush

2. Who is thought to have first established Aksum?

    A) King Menes B) King Ezana

    C) King Menelik, the son of King Solomon

3. What leader converted the kingdom to Christianity?

    A) King Ezana B) King Solomon C) Queen Cleopatra

4. What type of structure was Aksum famous for constructing?

    A) Pyramids B) Monuments C) Tall towers called steles

5. As well as their own language of Ge'ez, what other language was common?

    A) Latin B) Greek C) Arabic

Chapter 4 Answers

1. What is another common name for the Kingdom of Aksum?
   A) Axum
2. Who is thought to have first established Aksum?
   B) King Menelik, the son of King Solomon
3. What leader converted the kingdom to Christianity?
   A) King Ezana
4. What type of structure was Aksum famous for constructing?
   C) Tall towers called steles
5. As well as their own language of Ge'ez, what other language was common?
   B) Greek

Chapter 5: Medieval Africa

Many people mistakenly believe that Africa is a "dark continent" without much history, especially during the medieval period. However, this was not the case. The thousand-year medieval period (500 to 1500 CE) was a time of cultural, religious, and economic growth in Africa.

Fun Fact: It is estimated that Africa may have had up to ten thousand different states during the medieval period, each with its own language and culture!

At the start of the medieval period, Egypt had been under Roman rule since 30 CE. As well as introducing different cultures and using Egypt for trade, the Romans also introduced Christianity to the continent. After many years of fighting off Arab armies, the Romans eventually lost Egypt to them in 646. The new Arabic armies also brought their own religion: Islam.

During this time, the *Ghana Empire* was established, and new trade routes began to emerge around the Indian Ocean. The main items traded were slaves, gold, salt, and ivory. The demand for gold and salt was so high that a completely new trade route through the Sahara Desert was created. Before this, the Sahara Desert had been avoided due to its harsh climate. Because of the new trade route, new kingdoms emerged in this area in 700. These new states made trade even easier via this route.

From 500 to 1250 CE, ancient Ghana flourished as an organized society. It had a matrilineal monarchy and a system of law and order. It was reasonably wealthy due to its trade routes.

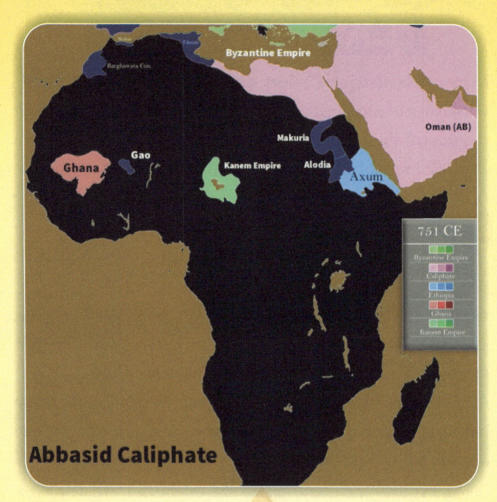

Map of medieval Africa, 751.

The next major kingdom during the medieval Africa period was the Kanem-Bornu Empire, which ran from the 9th century to the 19th century.

The *Mali Empire* began in 1235. It was in the same area as Ghana had been but went even farther along the *Niger River*. Most of the people in Mali lived in small villages. They worked as farmers or fishermen. Trade also flourished during this time, and Islam grew as a religion. Mali would have a *Mansa* as their ruler. He was chosen to rule by a council of leaders.

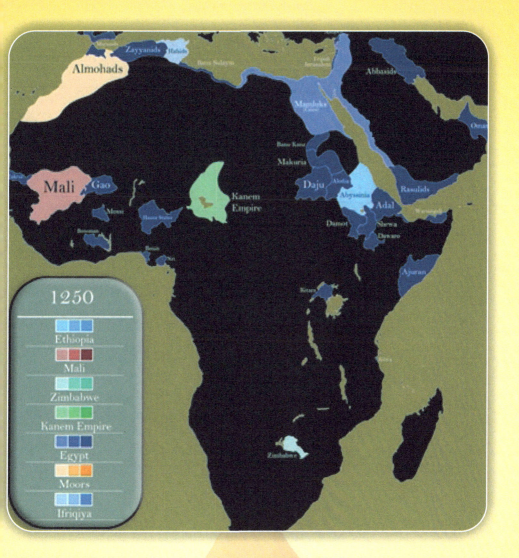

Map of medieval Africa, 1250

Around 1375, the state of *Gao*, which was based around a *tributary* (small stream or river that flows into a larger one) in Mali, broke away from Mali rule. This became the *Songhai Empire*.

Fun Fact: The leader of the Songhai Empire, *Sunni Ali*, managed to turn a very small town into a huge empire in just 28 years!

Map of medieval Africa, 1499

Because of the increased trade going on during the medieval period, African architecture began to flourish, as they were now rich enough to build with stone. In addition to building city walls, palaces, and houses, impressive churches and mosques were also built. In other, less affluent areas of Africa, buildings would be made from mudbrick.

Fun Fact: While Islam and Christianity were both growing in popularity in Africa throughout the Middle Ages, Christianity remained the major religion in Europe.

The Islamic people who had overthrown the Romans in North Africa decided to move away from the existing cities and start fresh. They built new cities nearby. Mosques dominated the cities. The capital of Egypt – Alexandria – moved and became *Fustat*, which is now called Cairo. Carthage moved to Tunisia, and a new city, *Kairouan*, was built in the desert there. Kairouan went on to be known as the fourth holiest city of Islam.

Fun Fact: The top three holiest cities of Islam are Mecca, Medina, and Jerusalem.

One of the most important buildings in Kairouan was the Great Mosque. It was built around 800 CE during the *Abbasid Caliphate*. A caliphate is similar to an empire. It is used to distinguish the states under Islamic rule. The Great Mosque was very impressive and far grander than anything being built in Europe at the time.

The Great Mosque of Kairouan, 670. Credit: Marek Szarejko, Wikimedia Commons
(https://commons.wikimedia.org/wiki/File:Great_Mosque_of_Kairouan_Panorama_-_Grande_Mosqu%C3%A9e_de_Kairouan_Panorama.jpg#/media/File:Great_Mosque_of_Kairouan_Panorama_-_Grande_Mosquée_de_Kairouan_Panorama.jpg)

The Great Mosque had several stone columns that were taken from existing Roman buildings. They decided to use the old columns rather than build new ones. They likely felt this move was symbolic of the Islamic defeat of the Romans.

At the Great Mosque, a *minaret* was also built. A minaret is a tower with stairs and an opening at the top. Islamic holy men would climb the minaret five times a day to announce the call to prayer (*muezzin*).

Fun Fact: The minaret at Kairouan was built in 700 CE. It is the oldest minaret still standing in the world!

Another impressive mosque built in this period was *the Great Mosque of Kilwa Kisiwani*. It was built during the 11th century. Kilwa Kisiwani is an island off the coast of Tanzania. At this time, Kilwa was a major port. It was vitally important to the success of the Indian Ocean trade route. Today, Kilwa Kisiwani is a UNESCO World Heritage Site.

Fun Fact: After the decline of Aksum, Kilwa was the first place south of the Sahara to mint gold coins.

The buildings at Kilwa Kisiwani were made from fossil coral limestone. For more decorative parts, they would use *porites*, a type of living stone-like coral. Mollusk shells, coral, and limestone would be crushed and combined with water to create white paint. When mixed with dirt or sand, this created a type of *mortar*.

The Great Mosque of Kilwa Kisiwani is an important part of African history. It is the oldest surviving mosque on the eastern coast of Africa. It is also one of the first mosques to have been built without a courtyard.

Fun Fact: While most mosques often only have one dome, the Great Mosque of Kilwa has an impressive sixteen domes!

The Great Mosque of Kilwa Kisiwani. Credit: Ron Van Oers, Wikimedia Commons
(https://commons.wikimedia.org/wiki/File:Ruins_of_Kilwa_Kisiwani_and_Ruins_of_Songo_Mnara-108279.jpg#/media/File:Ruins_of_Kilwa_Kisiwani_and_Ruins_of_Songo_Mnara-108279.jpg ;
https://commons.wikimedia.org/wiki/File:Inside_the_great_mosque_of_Kilwa.jpg#/media/File:Inside_the_great_mosque_of_Kilwa.jpg)

Inside the Great Mosque of Kilwa Kisiwani. Credit: Robin Chew, Wikimedia Commons
(https://commons.wikimedia.org/wiki/File:Inside_the_great_mosque_of_Kilwa.jpg#/media/File:Inside_the_great_mosque_of_Kilwa.jpg)

Another empire known for its architecture during this time was the *Ajuran Empire*. It was located in the Horn of Africa. The Ajuran Empire was predominantly Muslim and had a *theocratic* (religious) government. Many mosques were established throughout this empire, and most people converted to Islam. They also built many fortresses and castles.

Under the Ajuran *Sultanate* (a country run by a *sultan*), the small town of *Mogadishu* became the religious center of the empire. The wealthy and metropolitan city of Mogadishu was famous for its fine fabrics, which its merchants would trade all over the world via the Indian Ocean.

Fun Fact: Zheng He, a Chinese naval officer, was the first Chinese person to officially visit Africa. He went on a number of missions there during the 15th century, including to Mogadishu. He brought back the first African animals to China. The sultan of Mogadishu later visited and set up an embassy in China.

Just under twenty miles off the coast of Mogadishu is a small island in the Somali Sea. It contains many ruins that are typical of Ajuran architecture. One of these is the *Citadel* (fortress) of *Gondershe*.

The Citadel of Gondershe, Somalia
(https://commons.wikimedia.org/wiki/File:Gondereshe2008.jpg#/media/File:Gondereshe2008.jpg)

There were also many technological advancements during the Middle Ages in Africa. *Astronomy* (the scientific study of *celestial* objects in space) had been studied in Africa since the ancient Egyptians. Some significant discoveries happened in astronomy during the 12th to 16th centuries in Timbuktu.

One thing they believed in was *heliocentrism*. This means they thought the earth and other planets revolved around the sun. Many parts of the world at this time, especially Europe, believed that the opposite was true. They thought that the earth was the center of the universe, with the sun and other planets orbiting it.

They also used the *Julian calendar*, a calendar that was created by Julius Caesar. It is practically the same as the calendar still used in the Western world today. The main difference is that the Julian calendar had a leap year every three years. The one used today has a leap year every four years.

They also created impressive mathematical diagrams of the solar system, recorded astrological events, such as meteor showers, and calculated their exact location in relation to Mecca.

Fun Fact: Today, South Africa has many astronomers. It is home to the largest optical telescope in the Southern Hemisphere.

Africa also made medical advancements during the medieval period. Around the year 800 CE, the first hospital that specialized in caring for the mentally ill was built in Egypt. One would also be built in Baghdad around this time. The first mental asylum in Europe didn't open until 1247 in London. Not long after this, in 1285, Egypt went on to open the biggest hospital of the medieval period. Treatment was free to everyone. National healthcare was not established in Europe until 1948.

Fun Fact: In 1100 CE, the ventilator was invented in Egypt.

Chapter 5 Activities

Draw a line to connect the fact to its corresponding answer.

How often does the Julian calendar have a leap year?	The Arabs
Domes are a common feature in which type of building?	Europe
Zheng He took giraffes, hippos, ostriches, and more back to what country?	Mosques
The first psychological hospital was in what country?	Egypt
Christianity was the only dominant religion here during the Middle Ages.	3 years
Which people brought Islam to Africa?	China
What buildings do Christians worship in?	Churches

Chapter 5 Answers

Draw a line to connect the fact to its corresponding answer.

How often does the Julian calendar have a leap year?	3 years
Domes are a common feature in which type of building?	Mosques
Zheng He took giraffes, hippos, ostriches, and more back to what country?	China
The first psychological hospital was in what country?	Egypt
Christianity was the only dominant religion here during the Middle Ages.	Europe
Which people brought Islam to Africa?	The Arabs
What buildings do Christians worship in?	Churches

Chapter 6: The Ghana Empire

Now, we are going to learn more about the medieval African empires. First up is the *Ghana Empire*. It ran from approximately 300 to 1240 CE. The Ghana Empire was founded by several different tribes known as the *Soninke* people. They were united under the rule of the empire's first king, *Dinga Cisse*.

Fun Fact: The Ghana Empire is not to be confused with the modern-day Republic of Ghana, which is located in a different part of Africa. They are not related culturally.

The Ghana Empire was located in the west of Africa, where modern-day Mali, Senegal, and Mauritania now exist. Trade and transportation were made possible to the Ghana Empire thanks to the three main rivers in the area: the Niger River, Gambia River, and Senegal River.

Map of the Ghana Empire at its greatest extent.

Fun Fact: To travel to the Ghana Empire from the coast, you had to cross the Sahara Desert on camelback—this would take forty days on average!

Fun Fact: The Ghana Empire was actually referred to as *Wagadu* by its rulers. "Ghana" actually came from their word for king, *ghāna*.

The Ghana Empire was made up of several villages that were all under the rule of the ghāna. The ghāna was in control of many things, including the empire's justice system and religion. The people practiced *animism*. They believed that everything had a spiritual element and was alive. This included humans, animals, plants, rocks, weather, rivers, and so on. All of these elements were believed to have a direct interest in the lives of humans. They could help or hinder them. As the leader of this religion, the ghāna was treated with reverence. Sacrifices were made in his honor. When the ghāna died, he was buried on sacred land, which no one was allowed to enter.

During the Middle Ages, Islam became increasingly popular throughout Africa due to merchants from Arabic countries introducing Islam to the continent. However, the ghānas of the Ghana Empire did not convert to Islam.

While they did not fully convert to Islam, those who believed in the native religion and those who converted to Islam lived alongside each other. The capital city, *Koumbi Saleh*, was split in half. One side was Muslim, while the other believed in animism. The Muslim side of the city housed twelve mosques. Just over six miles away, on the other side of the capital, there was the palace and traditional shrines. This suggests that these two religions lived side by side in relative harmony.

When the ruins of Koumbi Saleh were discovered in 1913 by French archaeologists, they discovered a number of important artifacts, including *epigraphic shale plates* (a type of rock made into tablets with writing on them). These had religious inscriptions and geometric patterns on them.

Epigraphic shale plate from Koumbi Saleh. Credit: Clemens Schmillen, Wikimedia Commons
(https://commons.wikimedia.org/wiki/File:NouakchottNational Museum2.jpg#/media/File:NouakchottNationalMuseum2.jpg)

Another famous town in the Ghana Empire was *Chinguetti*. Like Koumbi Saleh, Chinguetti is now a UNESCO World Heritage Site. It has many fascinating ruins. The town was at the center of many of the trade routes. These trade routes helped the Ghana Empire grow to become powerful and wealthy.

In Chinguetti, the buildings are constructed from mudbrick and a reddish dry stone. The flat roofs were made from palm, while the doors were hand-cut from giant *acacia trees*. As well as a mosque, the town also had a fortress and a water tower. Chinguetti was home to five libraries that contained scientific and religious Islamic texts that date as far back as the Middle Ages.

Chinguetti, a town that was part of the Ghana Empire
(https://commons.wikimedia.org/wiki/File:Chinguetti-Vue_Goblale_Vieille_ ville.jpg#/media/File:Chinguetti-Vue_Goblale_Vieille_ville.jpg)

Fun Fact: The Ghana Empire was often nicknamed the "Land of Gold."

The rulers of the Ghana Empire also had control over the empire's immense wealth. One of the main trading commodities that the Ghana Empire possessed was its vast amount of gold.

Fun Fact: The ghāna stockpiled gold nuggets and forbade anyone from owning gold. Merchants were only permitted gold dust.

Forbidding others from owning gold nuggets meant that the ghāna could control the value of gold and make sure it didn't go down. If there was too much gold available at any given time, it would not be as valuable or desirable.

As well as an abundance of gold, the Ghana Empire also traded in other local resources. This included copper, ivory, and iron. Iron was used to create strong weapons and tools for their army.

Fun Fact: Metalworkers who made iron were considered to be magical since they used fire and earth to create something new.

Another desirable and highly valued commodity of the time was salt. Slaves would mine the salt from the Sahara Desert. If anyone wanted to trade salt, it would be subject to very high taxes. Salt was so valuable it could even be used as currency.

Fun Fact: Salt was worth the same as gold!

The decline of the Ghana Empire began for several reasons. Climate change factored in when unusually dry weather occurred. Also, new trade routes that were farther east and easier for merchants to get to began to become more popular, cutting off their once-lucrative trade deals.

On top of this, a group of Muslim *Berber* tribes known as the *Almoravids* began a holy crusade to convert people to Islam. When the rulers of the Ghana Empire refused to convert, civil wars broke out between the two religions. This led to economic instability. Many tribal chiefs took advantage of the chaos and established independent kingdoms.

Over a period of hundreds of years, the Ghana Empire began to disintegrate. In 1240, it became part of the Mali Empire.

Chapter 6 Activities

True or false?

1. The Ghana Empire was founded by Emperor Mansa.
2. The capital of the Kingdom of Ghana was Koumbi Saleh.
3. Dinga Cisse was the first king of the newly formed empire.
4. After its fall, the Ghana Empire became a part of the Kanem-Bornu Empire.
5. Only the king was allowed to own gold nuggets.
6. The Ghana Empire would take one hundred days to reach on camelback from the coast. There was only one religion in the Ghana Empire.
7. The Ghana Empire was actually referred to as Wagadu.

Chapter 6 Answers

True or false?

1. The Ghana Empire was founded by Emperor Mansa. – False
   It was founded when a group of tribes united under King Dinga Cisse.
2. The capital of the Kingdom of Ghana was Koumbi Saleh. – True
3. Dinga Cisse was the first king of the newly formed empire. – True
4. After its fall, the Ghana Empire became a part of the Kanem-Bornu Empire. – False
   It became part of the Mali Empire.
5. Only the king was allowed to own gold nuggets. – True
6. The Ghana Empire would take one hundred days to reach on camelback from the coast. – False
   On average, it took forty days.
7. There was only one religion in the Ghana Empire. – False
   Islam and animism were the two main religions.
8. The Ghana Empire was actually referred to as Wagadu. – True

Chapter 7: The Kanem-Bornu Empire

Our journey through African history has now led us to the time when the *Kanem-Bornu Empire* reigned supreme. The Kanem-Bornu Empire was based around *Lake Chad*. It spanned modern-day Chad, Nigeria, Cameroon, Niger, and Libya.

Fun Fact: When it was first founded, it was known as the Kanem Empire. Bornu was added later.

Around 700 CE, *Kanem* was settled by the previously nomadic *Zaghawa* or *Kanembu* people. Its first ruling family was from the *Duguwa Dynasty*. However, the Kanembu people did not discover Kanem. It was already occupied by the *Sao culture*. Historians think the Sao civilization could have been there since as early as 600 BCE.

Fun Fact: The occupation was not amicable. A civil war went on between the Sao and Kanembu people until the 16th century.

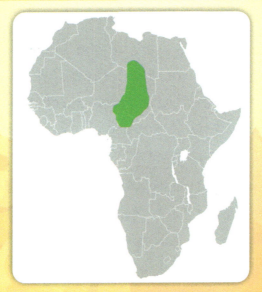

Map of the Kanem-Bornu Empire
(https://commons.wikimedia.org/wiki/File:Kanem-Bornu.svg)

The existing walled cities built by the Sao and fertile lands were the main reasons that the Kanembu decided to settle in Kanem. They created a new city, *N'jimi* (which meant "south"). This city became the capital.

In 1023, the Kanem Empire expanded into the Sahara Desert under the rule of *King Arku*. By taking over this area, they also gained control of the trade routes. This trade provided the empire with wealth. It also meant that the people of Kanem were introduced to Islam.

Fun Fact: The main items that the Kanembu people traded were slaves, ostrich feathers, and ivory.

The next *mai* (ruler) was important for two reasons. Firstly, this might have been the first female queen of the empire. However, it is not known for sure if this particular ruler was male or female. More importantly, this was the first mai to convert to Islam. This ruler was known as Hu or Hawwa. They only reigned for four years (1067-1071). Their successors were also Muslim.

After over three hundred years of the Duguwa Dynasty, a new dynasty appeared. This was the *Sefuwa Dynasty*. It was formed around 1075. The Sefuwa Dynasty was one of the longest in African history. It ran until 1846. It was one of the most important Muslim kingdoms in Africa during this period.

The Sefuwa Dynasty not only had its own land. It was also in charge of twelve other states. On top of expanding the empire, the Sefuwa Dynasty also managed to gain control of the valuable salt mines in Bilma. They would use the salt to trade for glass, horses, and fabric. The horses they traded for were especially vital for the expansion of the empire. This was because their soldiers would ride into battle on horseback. *Mai Dunama Dibalami* was responsible for further expanding the empire during his reign. He ruled from 1210 until 1248. This expansion was largely thanks to his army of forty thousand men and horses.

A group of Kanem warriors
(https://commons.wikimedia.org/wiki/File:Group_of_Kanem-Bu_warriors.jpg)

At the start of 1500, Kanem became known as Kanem-Bornu. This is because, in the 14th century, the *Bulala people* of Chad forced the *mai* to abandon the capital and move it to an area called *Bornu*. Fortunately, the move to Bornu was successful. It was more fertile there. This led to new trade deals with the *Hausa Kingdoms* in modern-day Nigeria. By 1497, *Mai Ali Ghaji* was powerful enough to recapture Kanem, and the kingdom began to be known as the Kanem-Bornu Empire.

Fun Fact: The Kanem-Bornu Empire wasn't officially known as this until 1617, when the Kanem and Bornu regions were unified.

Mai Idris Alooma ruled from 1564 to 1596. He was one of the most successful mais and was known for his military prowess. He reportedly fought and won over 1,000 battles and 330 wars. He came up with new military tactics, such as building walls around battle camps, using armor for soldiers and horses, and *scorched-earth tactics*. This means the soldiers destroyed anything that the enemy needed, such as land, housing, and food. He also introduced camels from the Sahara to replace the less suitable oxen and donkeys that were being used.

Idris Alooma was a devout Muslim. He went on a *pilgrimage* (a spiritual journey) in 1571 to the Islamic holy land, Mecca. He encouraged his people to do the same. He also improved the justice system by appointing qualified officials to uphold the law.

The Kanem-Bornu Empire did not last long once the Sefuwa Dynasty ended. In 1893, the empire was overthrown by *Rabih az-Zubayr* from Sudan. He did not remain in control of the empire for long. European forces soon arrived, and the land was divided and conquered.

A depiction of a young woman from Bornu
(https://commons.wikimedia.org/wiki/File:Young_woman_from_Bornu.jpg)

The rulers and noblemen would wear wool and cotton. The people of Kanem-Bornu would mostly wear clothing made from crocodile or leopard skin.

In the Kanem-Bornu Empire, people had jobs that were similar to those elsewhere in Africa. The lower-class people would be slaves, soldiers, or farmers. Farming was considered an important job, and the workers were paid. They would grow wheat, beans, and a common type of ancient grain called *millet*. Artisans and merchants were also important jobs since they helped grow the wealth of the kingdom and traded for valuable goods.

The highest position for noblemen was to be in the government. The mai would ask them for help when making any decisions.

Fun Fact: The two highest positions in the government were held by women—the queen mother and queen sister.

The Kanem-Bornu Empire was made up of many different states. They all had their own unique customs, but they shared the same religion, language, and culture. Some cities were so big that they became capitals themselves. They would be in control of hundreds of nearby villages. Each city-state was controlled by a council of important members of society. This included the rulers, the head of the police, and the chief of finance.

Fun Fact: The biggest city-states were home to over 100,000 people at their peak.

The flag of the Bornu Empire
(https://commons.wikimedia.org/wiki/File:Flag_of_the_Bornu_Empire.svg#/media/File:Flag_of_the_Bornu_Empire.svg)

Chapter 7 Activities

Oh, no! The timeline of the Kanem-Bornu Empire is all jumbled up below. Can you reorder the events correctly?

1. The reign of King Idris Alooma began.
2. The empire was founded by the Zaghawa or Kanembu nomadic people.
3. The Kanem Empire expanded into the Sahara.
4. The Kanem-Bornu Empire was taken over by Sudan.
5. Bornu recaptured the lost territories and became the Kanem-Bornu Empire.
6. Islam was adopted as the state religion.
7. The Sefuwa Dynasty began.

Chapter 7 Answers

1. The empire was founded by the Zaghawa or Kanembu nomadic people.
2. The Kanem Empire expanded into the Sahara.
3. Islam was adopted as the state religion.
4. The Sefuwa Dynasty began.
5. Bornu recaptured the lost territories and became the Kanem-Bornu Empire.
6. The reign of King Idris Alooma began.
7. The Kanem-Bornu Empire was taken over by Sudan.

Chapter 8: The Mali Empire

We are going to learn more about another medieval African empire. This one is the *Mali Empire*. It was formed around 1235 CE by *Sundiata Keita*. He united lots of smaller *Malinké* kingdoms that were located in the west of Africa around the Niger River.

Fun Fact: The Disney film, The Lion King, is thought to be loosely based on Sundiata Keita's life.

Sundiata Keita was nicknamed "Lion King" because his name was derived from the word *jata*, which means "lion." Sundiata's father, King *Maghan*, was married to a beautiful woman. His first son was named *Dankaran Touman*. However, the king was told in a prophecy that if he remarried an ugly woman, their son would be the true heir to the kingdom.

When the king's second "ugly" wife gave birth to Sundiata, Maghan was disappointed to find the boy was weak and crippled. He believed the prophecy would not be fulfilled, but he still loved him very much.

The first wife was jealous. She wanted her son to be the king, not Sundiata. She got her wish. When Sundiata was only three years old, his father died. His half-brother, Touman, became king. Touman and his mother were cruel to Sundiata and teased him.

Touman was not in power for long. He was overthrown by the *Sosso people*. Sundiata became a prisoner of the Sosso. As he got older, he grew stronger and began to walk. Once he was old enough, Sundiata fled into exile. While he was away, he became a powerful warrior. Eventually, he was convinced to return home and claim his kingdom.

Sundiata returned with an army and fought a number of battles against the Sosso. He had the support of his people, who were happy to see their prophesized king return. In the *Battle of Kirina*, Sundiata fought against the Sosso leader, *Soumaoro*. Sundiata was victorious. He defeated Soumaoro with a poisoned arrow. With their king gone, the Sosso people were easy to topple, and Sundiata regained his birthright. He then went on to expand the Mali Empire. He named a new city, *Niani*, as its capital.

Fun Fact: Sundiata was the first Mali ruler to use the term *Mansa*, which means "king of kings."

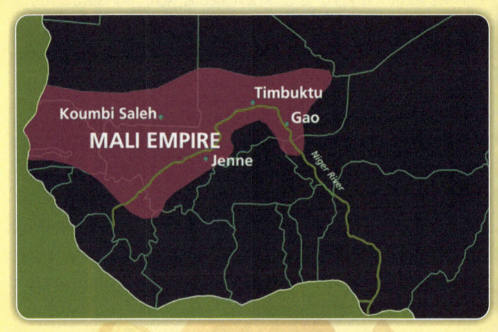

Map of the Mali Empire at its greatest extent.

The Mali Empire was at its most powerful with its ninth ruler, *Mansa Musa*. He was the king from 1312 to 1337. His huge empire spanned across nine modern-day African countries: Mali, Niger, Nigeria, Mauritania, Gambia, Guinea, Burkina Faso, Senegal, and Chad.

Fun Fact: Mansa Musa became king because his predecessor went missing! *Muhammad ibn Qu* went on an expedition with two thousand ships to explore the Atlantic Ocean, but he never returned.

When Mansa Musa took over, the Mali Empire was already very rich and powerful. He doubled the empire's land during his rule so that it stretched over two thousand miles. This made it even wealthier, as they gained access to even more trade routes. The three main sources of wealth for the Mali Empire were ivory, gold, and salt.

Fun Fact: It is believed that Mansa Musa may have been the richest person of all time! He was so rich that it cannot even be calculated how much he owned.

In 1324, Mansa Musa decided he was going to go on a pilgrimage to Mecca. But as you might expect for the richest man who ever lived, he did it in style. He reportedly traveled there with sixty thousand people, including twelve thousand slaves who catered to his every whim. He also took a caravan of one hundred camels. They each carried three hundred pounds of gold!

Because the gold was so heavy, his camels couldn't carry it past Cairo. So, he gave the sultan of Egypt enormous amounts of gold. He gave away so much gold that the overall value of gold dropped in Egypt. It took twelve years to go back up! This caused widespread economic devastation. Mansa Musa's huge amounts of gold soon meant that the Mali Empire was known all over the world for its impressive wealth.

Fun Fact: Mansa Musa was quite literally "on the map." In 1375, a Spanish *cartographer* (mapmaker) created the first European map of West Africa. On it, Mansa Musa was drawn holding a gold nugget and wearing a golden crown.

Mansa Musa brought a number of respected scholars, poets, and architects back home. One of these architects was paid a whopping 440 pounds of gold, which today is worth over eight million dollars! This architect is said to have designed the impressive *Djinguereber Mosque* in Timbuktu.

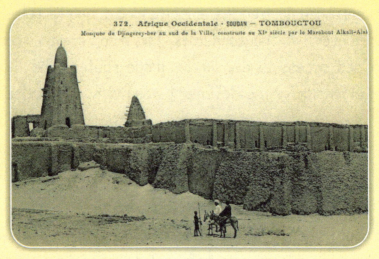

Djinguereber Mosque in Timbuktu
(https://commons.wikimedia.org/wiki/File:Fortier_372_Timbuktu_Djingereber_Mosque.jpg#/media/File:Fortier_372_Timbuktu_Djingereber_Mosque.jpg)

Djinguereber Mosque in Timbuktu
(https://commons.wikimedia.org/wiki/File:Fortier_368_Timbuktu_Sankore_Mosque.jpg#/media/File:Fortier_368_Timbuktu_Sankore_Mosque.jpg)

Mansa Musa also used his great wealth to revitalize the Mali Empire's cities, such as Timbuktu and Gao. Under his rule, Timbuktu became renowned as a cultural center for learning. Its Islamic university became a popular choice for scholars from all over the world to come and study.

Because the Mali Empire was so big, it contained many different cultures and religions. Although Mansa Musa was Muslim, he did not force his religion onto his subjects. He also split the empire into different areas. Each had its own *farba* (governor). They were in charge of keeping the peace in their area and paying taxes and tribute to the Mansa.

After Mansa Musa's death in 1337, the Mali Empire had several different rulers. Many of them contributed to the empire's gradual decline. In 1360, *Mansa Mari Djata II* nearly bankrupted the empire due to his extravagant spending. He did maintain good relationships with Morocco. He even sent a giraffe as a gift for the king! Luckily, Mari Djata II did not live long enough to completely bankrupt the empire. He died in 1374.

In spite of Mari Djata's spending, the empire still continued for many more years under numerous rulers. Over the years, the empire continued to weaken. In the early 1430s, it even lost its famous city of Timbuktu to the *Tuareg*. Timbuktu was then conquered again in 1468 by the Songhai Empire. It had taken one of the Mali Empire's oldest areas of land, *Mema*, three years earlier. The Songhai Empire went on to take over the valuable salt and copper mines from the Mali Empire.

The last ruler of the Mali Empire was *Mansa Mahmud IV*. In 1599, he unsuccessfully tried to take control of the neighboring city of *Djenne*, which had never been part of the Mali Empire before. Unfortunately, he was unable to capture the city. When Mahmud IV died in 1610, his three sons fought over who would take over. None of them ever had full control. Instead, they divided the empire into three, ending the once-great Mali Empire for good.

The Great Mosque of Djenne. Credit: Andy Gilham, Wikimedia Commons.
(https://commons.wikimedia.org/wiki/File:Great_Mosque_of_Djenn%C3%A9_1.jpg#/media/File:Great_Mosque_of_Djenné_1.jpg)

Chapter 8 Activities

Can you match the Mansa with his achievements?

Mansa Mahmud IV	United the tribes of the Malinké peoples and formed the Mali Empire
Mansa Sundiata Keita	Developed cities like Timbuktu and Gao into important cultural centers and improved the Mali Empire
Mansa Musa	Maintained a good relationship with Morocco
Mansa Mari Djata II	Launched an attack on the city of Djenne that failed

Chapter 8 Answers

Mansa Sundiata Keita	United the tribes of the Malinké peoples and formed the Mali Empire
Mansa Musa	Developed cities like Timbuktu and Gao into important cultural centers and improved the Mali Empire
Mansa Mari Djata II	Maintained a good relationship with Morocco
Mansa Mahmud IV	Launched an attack on the city of Djenne that failed

Chapter 9: Colonization and Enslavement

Toward the end of the Middle Ages, things took a sad turn for Africa and its people. From the 16th century to the 19th century, Africa began to be colonized and enslaved by Western civilizations. Although slavery was still being practiced by the African people, it was less prevalent in the Western world by this point. But even before the official colonization began, Western invaders had been taking slaves back with them. When the Portuguese came in 1442, they began taking African slaves home with them.

However, we tend to think of the transatlantic slave trade as beginning in 1502. This was when the Spanish needed to replace the native slaves in the Caribbean and American colonies. They decided to import slaves from Africa. In 1518, King Charles I of Spain gave permission to the slave traders to directly take African slaves to the Americas instead of having to go through European ports first. This meant that the slave trade began to increase in volume. And there was a great demand for new slaves since the native slaves in the Americas were dying from European diseases and warfare.

The English, Dutch, French, and Danish also began to colonize the West Indies. They decided to replace their existing workforce of poor white people with African slaves.

The first English slave-trading voyage happened in 1562. It was led by *John Hawkins*. The British didn't trade large numbers of slaves until the first English colonies in the Americas were established in the 17th century. During this century, the demand for slaves to work on sugar and tobacco plantations increased, so more slaves were imported.

Book with names, ages, and other details of the slaves
(https://commons.wikimedia.org/wiki/File:Jefferson_slaves.jpg)

By studying the ship logs and manifests that detail the slaves being exported from Africa and sold, historians have been able to estimate that almost twelve million Africans were forcibly removed from their homeland during the transatlantic slave trade. However, as many as 15 to 25 percent of the captured people would not survive the long voyage across the Atlantic Ocean.

More than two million people died on the journey to the Americas due to the dangerous conditions on the boats.

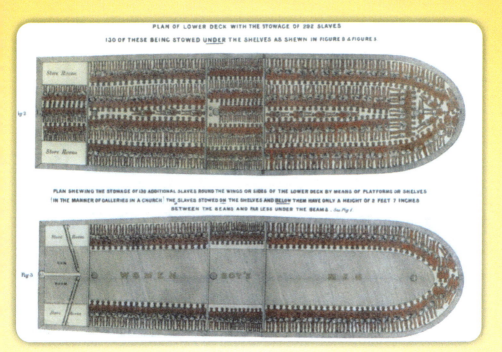

Standard slave ship

The journey across the Atlantic was referred to as *the Middle Passage*. It was about five thousand miles long, which meant it could take several months for ships to reach their destination. The journey was horrific.

The captured African people would be crammed into dirty boats. Men were often chained together so they could not *mutiny* (uprise against the captain). Families would be separated from one another. They were barely allowed up onto the deck to see the sunlight since the crew feared they would uprise.

Below deck, the low ceilings meant they couldn't even sit up straight. Each person had a space of around six feet long, sixteen inches wide, and three feet high. This means they couldn't move or turn over very easily. It was very hot on the ship. Since there were so many people packed on board, there often was not enough oxygen for even candles to stay lit for long.

The length of the journey would often make the difference between life and death. On longer voyages, food would run out. It would then be rationed, with the crew getting priority. Diseases from poor sanitation were also rife.

The ship's crew treated the captured people horrifically. They were very cruel, as they believed that the Africans were less than human. In 1781, the *Zong* suffered problem after problem. Disease spread through the ship, and they encountered bad weather. They were behind schedule, and clean water became an issue. The captain ordered 130 slaves to be thrown overboard to try to save water. Because the slaves were seen as property and not people, he filed an insurance claim for the loss of the money he would have made selling them.

A drawing of slaves on board a ship

Sometimes, the African slaves on ships were able to successfully overthrow the captain. In 1839, a captured slave, *Joseph Cinqué*, led 53 other captives to mutiny against the ship. It was later ordered by the US Supreme Court that the freed slaves should be returned home.

Britain and Portugal were the two biggest slave-trading countries. They were responsible for importing around 70 percent of the slaves. Not everyone in Britain was happy with the slave trade. Some people petitioned for it to be banned for over twenty years before it was finally *abolished* (formally ended). The Slave Trade Act was passed on March 25th, 1807. The United States then followed suit, outlawing the slave trade in 1808.

However, while new slaves could not be imported, owning existing slaves was still permitted. In 1838, the British finally *emancipated* (freed) their 800,000 slaves. Shockingly, in order to free the slaves, the British government also agreed to pay over 26 million dollars in compensation to the plantation owners. The ex-slaves were given nothing for their years of servitude!

It wasn't until 1865 that the United States outlawed slavery. This happened two years after President Abraham Lincoln issued the *Emancipation Proclamation*. The Thirteenth Amendment to the US Constitution abolished slavery, stating that "Neither slavery nor involuntary servitude, except as a punishment for crime whereof the party shall have been duly convicted, shall exist within the United States, or any place subject to their jurisdiction."

The slave trade had a devastating impact on the countries, cultures, and people of Africa. With so many people being forcibly removed (an estimated 25 million between the transatlantic Slave Trade and the

Arabic slave trade), the population and economy of Africa struggled to grow and develop. Because of this, it also paved the way for the colonization of Africa.

A picture of the French cavalry in what is now South Africa
(https://commons.wikimedia.org/wiki/File:French%27s_Cavalry_at_Klip_Drift.jpg)

While foreigners had been coming to Africa for many years, it wasn't until after 1880 that the European colonization of Africa began. Prior to this, most of Africa's interior had been unexplored by Western powers due to disease and difficult travel routes. Ninety percent of Africa was still under African control.

However, in 1884, the *Berlin Conference* was held. It was decided how Africa would be divided among the colonial powers (Britain, France, Belgium, Spain, Portugal, and Germany). Other countries, such as Denmark and the United States, were also involved in the conference, but they went home empty-handed.

Fun Fact: This period is often nicknamed the "Scramble for Africa" since the colonizing powers quite literally scrambled around trying to get their portion of the continent.

There were many reasons why the colonial powers wanted to claim parts of Africa for themselves. Firstly, the more countries under their control, the more powerful they would be. Their power would be known around the world. There was also an economic *depression* going on in Europe. This means the economy was not doing as well as it should. Africa's abundance of natural resources made it an incredibly appealing place to own.

To overcome the big issue of travel, the European colonizers built railways and steamboats that could travel along the African rivers.

The African people did not simply allow invaders to take over their land. They often fought back against Western control. Sadly, most would lose the fight and fall under the control of the invading Europeans. However, Italy was unsuccessful in taking over Ethiopia. The Ethiopians won the fight for their land in 1896.

Fun Fact: The European colonizers wanted to focus on bringing the "three Cs" to Africa: Christianity, commerce, and European civilization.

A Christian revival was under way in Europe. This meant that there were lots of European missionaries who wanted to preach the word of God. They wanted to convert the largely

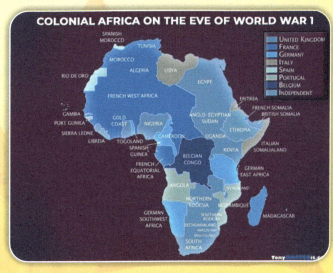

Map of colonized Africa in 1914

Muslim and tribal people of Africa to Christianity.

By the 1900s, a huge portion of Africa had been colonized. The Europeans were able to take control quickly since they took advantage of the rivalries between African leaders. Nature also played a part. In 1895, a severe drought, a plague of locusts, and a cattle plague all meant that there was not enough food. The Africans were too weak to fight back. The invading Europeans also had far better weapons, such as the machine gun. There was also a smallpox *epidemic* (the rapid spread of a disease within a localized region) that wiped out many of the Africans. It did not affect the Europeans as much. They had some *immunity* (resistance to diseases) from previous European epidemics.

The European powers then set about establishing colonial states that were very strict and *authoritarian*. This meant that the African people had no input into how their new colony was run. They also deliberately weakened the indigenous institutions. The colonial powers did not properly fund the colonies, which means there was little in the way of infrastructure.

Fun Fact: The contribution of African people to the war effort during World War I was integral and yet is often ignored.

Chapter 9 Activities

1. Who are the European colonial powers?
2. When did the Slave Trade Act pass? In which country?
3. What happened after the Berlin Conference of 1884?
4. Which amendment ended slavery in the United States?

Chapter 9 Answers

1. Who are the European colonial powers? Britain, France, Belgium, Spain, Portugal, and Germany.

2. When did the Slave Trade Act pass? In which country? 1807 in Britain.

3. What happened after the Berlin Conference of 1884? Africa was divided up between the European colonial powers.

4. Which amendment ended slavery in the United States? The Thirteenth Amendment.

Chapter 10: Decolonization and Independence

During the 20th century, there were many *African independence movements*. These happened when the African people revolted against colonial rule. In 1946, a group of politicians in the French-occupied area of West Africa formed a new political party known as the *African Democratic Rally* or *RDA*. It played a vital role in the *decolonization* (ending colonialism) of the French Empire.

Meanwhile, in 1948, in British-occupied West Africa, boycotts and riots took place. It was later decided that the African people should have a greater say in government matters with the aim of eventually becoming self-governing nations. In 1951, a new constitution was brought in, and newly elected African leaders became responsible for running the government.

Fun Fact: In 1957 CE, Ghana became the first African country to declare independence from colonial rule.

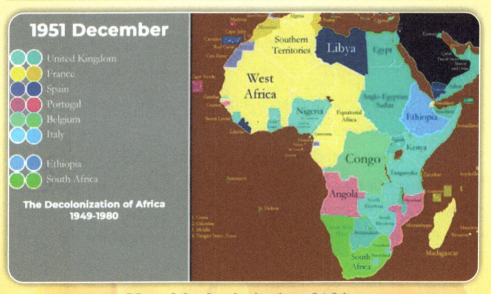

Map of the decolonization of Africa

From 1954 to 1962, *the Algerian War for Independence* took place. The fight for independence from the French had been going on since the First World War. But after the Second World War, the French had still failed to fulfill their promise of giving Algeria more control. So, the *National Liberation Front* began a *guerrilla war* (small and fast movements against military and police forces) against the French. Finally, in 1962, Algeria gained its independence.

In 1963, Kenya also gained its independence from British rule. In the previous decade, there was a massive uprising known as the *Mau Mau Uprising*. The uprising cost the British over seventy million dollars. They were brutal to the Kenyans. They killed civilians and forced many people into concentration camps. The uprising made the British realize things needed to change, and reforms began being introduced. The independence agreement stated that the government would be made up of 66 seats. Thirty-three of those would go to Black Kenyans, twenty would go to other ethnic groups, and the rest to the British.

Fun Fact: The first prime minister of Kenya was *Jomo Kenyatta*, who had been falsely imprisoned by the British following the Mau Mau Uprising.

Although Egypt technically became an independent country in 1922, the British maintained a strong influence over it for many years afterward. Much to the annoyance of the Egyptians, who believed the valuable Suez Canal should be theirs, the British maintained control of it. In 1956, the *Egyptian Nationalist* leader, *Abdel Nasser*, took it from the British and French. This led to a fight for the canal. The British and French were heavily criticized by the United States and other countries for this. Britain was pressured into giving the canal back to Egypt. This was a sure sign that the once-great colonial power of Britain had ended.

South Africa was another country that had a long road to independence. While it technically became independent in 1931, the British *monarch* (king or queen) was still in charge. It wasn't until 1961 that South Africa was declared an independent nation. However, South Africa was still under a racist *apartheid* regime at this time.

Apartheid was a system that favored white people over black people. It enforced *segregation* (the separation of different racial groups. Under apartheid, black people could not own land, own or run a business, or live in certain areas. Marriage or relationships between different races were illegal. Education was skewed. Black students were taught manual skills, and they were unable to attend university. Other laws were introduced that allowed the police to use extreme force and even torture or kill people while on duty. Political uprisings were also strictly monitored. Anyone who seemed to be speaking out would be arrested.

The people still protested, even though it was banned. On March 21st, 1960, a protest against apartheid took place in *Sharpeville*. The police shot into the crowd, and 69 Black South Africans were killed.

Many other countries around the world did not accept the South African regime. It left the British Commonwealth in 1961. It became a republic, but the African people still had no real say. This led civil rights activist *Nelson Mandela* to launch a campaign against apartheid. Mandela's political activism led to him being sentenced to life in prison in 1964. Over the next twenty years, rising pressure from outside countries led South Africa to slowly begin changing its laws from 1986 onward.

Fun Fact: Nelson Mandela was released in 1990 after serving 27 years in prison!

On April 26th, 1994, adults from all races were able to vote in elections. A coalition government, with a black majority and Nelson Mandela as the president, came into effect. This date is now known as "Freedom Day" in South Africa. This led to the end of apartheid. However, many racist and separatist ideals still exist in the country today.

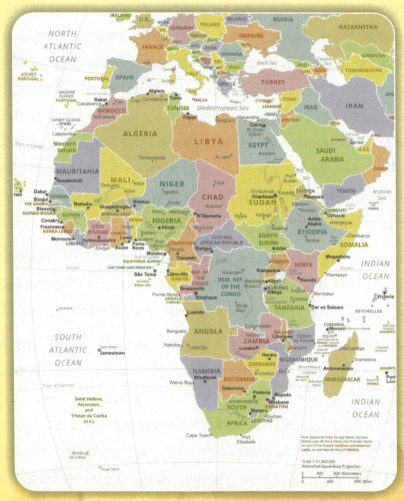

Map of present-day Africa
(https://commons.wikimedia.org/wiki/File:Political_Map_of_Africa.svg)

Fun Fact: Nelson Mandela was the first black president of South Africa.

Colonialism and European colonization had a devastating impact on the people and economy of Africa. However, today, Africa is thriving. It has one of the fastest-growing economies in the world. In fact, the overall economy of Africa has gone up by over 400 percent in the past twenty years.

Access to education is improving too. From 2000 to 2020, the number of children attending high school increased by 150 percent!

Fun Fact: In the past twenty years, life expectancy in Africa has gone up by almost eleven years!

Africa is also leading the way when it comes to climate change initiatives and green energy, even though it only uses 2 percent of the world's coal. Morocco has built the world's largest solar panel farm. They aim to use 52 percent of renewable energy by 2030. The complex not only provides clean energy for two million people. It also provides jobs for the community. South Africa has introduced a carbon tax that could improve their emissions by 33 percent by 2030. Many other countries in Africa are also introducing similar initiatives.

Now that the African people have control of their homeland, advancements like these will hopefully keep happening, and the continent will continue to thrive.

Chapter 10 Activities

Can you match the words/phrases to their meaning?

Independence	Formally ended.
Apartheid	Settling of land and controlling the indigenous/native people of an area.
Decolonization	Small and fast movements against military and police forces.
Colonization	The ability for the country to govern and control itself.
Abolish	A system that favored white people over black people and enforced segregation of the races.
Guerilla war	Ending of colonial control.

Chapter 10 Answers

Independence	The ability for the country to govern and control itself.
Apartheid	A system that favored white people over black people and enforced segregation of the races.
Decolonization	Ending of colonial control.
Colonization	Settling of land and controlling the indigenous/native people of an area.
Abolish	Formally ended.
Guerilla war	Small and fast movements against military and police forces.

Part 2:

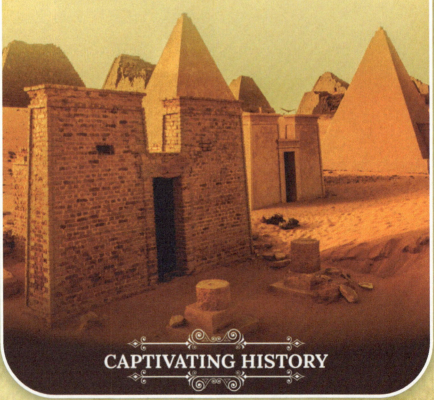

ANCIENT AFRICA FOR KIDS

A CAPTIVATING GUIDE TO ANCIENT AFRICAN CIVILIZATIONS, EMPIRES, AND HISTORY

CAPTIVATING HISTORY

INTRODUCTION

Did you know that historians believe the first people came from Africa? This continent has been essential to the development of the world as we know it. There were many different tribes and civilizations in Africa, and some of these ancient civilizations were so powerful that lots of people traveled to them.

But what were these early African civilizations? How did their people live? The history of ancient Africa is filled with fighting armies, wealthy nations, and amazing buildings. They made beautiful art and followed their religious beliefs devoutly to enjoy the afterlife. Both students and parents will enjoy reading this fun, up-to-date history of the civilizations of ancient Africa.

In this book, you'll learn all about the rise and fall of the great Kingdom of Kerma. Kerma eventually became Kush, which became both a friend and an enemy of ancient Egypt. You'll also learn about the wealthy kingdom of Aksum and Ghana, which wasn't anywhere near the nation of Ghana today.

This book has all the information you need to explore early African history. Get ready to dig in and learn how ancient Africa shaped the world around us today.

Chapter 1: The Kingdom of Kerma

Although it no longer exists today, the **Kingdom of Kerma** was once one of the most powerful civilizations in Africa. It was located in modern-day northern Sudan and southern Egypt. It lasted from 2500 BCE to 1500 BCE. That's one thousand years! The kingdom is named after **Kerma**, which is the main city archaeologists have found so far. Its biggest achievement was conquering a big part of the Upper Kingdom of Egypt. The people of Kerma were known for being fantastic archers.

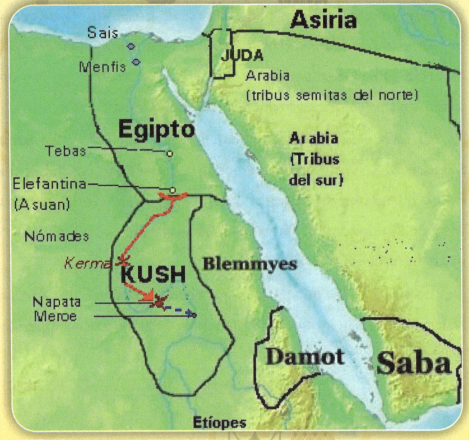

A map showing the location of the Kerma culture along the Nile.
Quijav, CC BY-SA 4.0 https://creativecommons.org/licenses/by-sa/4.0 via Wikimedia Commons
https://commons.wikimedia.org/wiki/File:Kush-591aC.png

The Kingdom of Kerma didn't just appear out of nowhere, though. Building a civilization like that takes time. Archaeologists believe that people lived along the Nile River in the area as long ago as 5000 BCE. Those first people built villages and trading places. Before long, they were building bigger villages and even cities. They began to conquer more of **Nubia**, which was the area they were in. Eventually, the city of Kerma became the most powerful, and the Kingdom of Kerma took over Nubia in 2500 BCE.

Although the Kingdom of Kerma would eventually be as big as Egypt, its capital would be the heart of its power. For that time in history, the city was big. Many people lived in the city, and it also had a large cemetery.

Archaeologists know that Kerma had a complex social system. While some ancient civilizations had strict divisions between royalty, merchants, and farmers, Kerma seems to have been more diverse.

A picture of what the city of Kerma looks like today.
Lassi, CC BY-SA 4.0 https://creativecommons.org/licenses/by-sa/4.0 via Wikimedia Commons; https://commons.wikimedia.org/wiki/File:Kerma_city.JPG

The cemetery reveals that many people had big funeral services. Other civilizations would reserve such displays for royalty, but Kerma appears to have allowed anyone to have a magnificent funeral as long as they could afford it.

Archaeologists have not found many other cities in the Kingdom of Kerma. However, there were many villages. The farming and fishing villages seem to have been the most important part of Kerma. They sustained the kingdom and helped it become wealthy. The kingdom was split into regions that were ruled by governors called **pestos**. Each pesto had people who reported to him, so the political structure appears to have been complex.

The Kingdom of Kerma lasted for one thousand years. Historians divide the kingdom into three periods. The first period is called **Ancient** or **Early Kerma**, and it lasted from 2500 BCE to 2050 BCE. The second period is called **Middle Kerma**, and it lasted from 2050 BCE to 1750 BCE. The last period is called **Classic Kerma**, and it lasted from 1750 BCE to 1500 BCE.

The Egyptians and the people of Kerma both traded and fought with each other throughout the Ancient Kerma and Middle Kerma periods. They were both powerful enough that their fights didn't really change anything, but their trading helped both civilizations become more prosperous.

All of that changed around 1750 BCE. In 1786 BCE, Egypt was attacked from the north by the **Hyksos** (hik-sôs). They were strong and took over most of the **Lower Kingdom**, which was the northern half of Egypt. Although Kerma was a trading ally with Egypt, the people saw this as a chance to expand the kingdom. They made an alliance with the Hyksos and were allowed to conquer the **Upper Kingdom**, which was the southern half of Egypt. Egypt wasn't completely destroyed, but they were reduced to a small city called Thebes.

The Kingdom of Kerma had its golden age while ruling over the Upper Kingdom. They also took over the Sudanese Kingdom of Sai, so they had a lot of new land and wealth to use. Although they were still very dependent on agriculture, the Classic Kerma period was the height of the kingdom's wealth and power. Everyone who traveled to trade used certain roads and rivers. Kerma had control of the route that went from East Africa to West Africa. They also controlled the route that went between Central Africa and the Mediterranean Sea. They were able to collect a lot of money by charging taxes, similar to our toll roads today.

What ancient Kerma pottery looks like.
Sue Fleckney, CC BY-SA 2.0 https://creativecommons.org/licenses/by-sa/2.0 via Wikimedia Commons; https://commons.wikimedia.org/wiki/File:Pottery_Kerma_Museum,_Kerma,_Sudan,_North-east_Africa.jpg

The people of Kerma didn't just farm and trade. They also made pottery and metal pieces. They even built monuments called **deffufas** (de-fuf-fa). There were at least three in the Kingdom of Kerma. These were tall structures built from mud bricks that were piled on top of each other to create unique shapes. Archaeologists think they were temples or used for funeral services. The inside walls were usually decorated with tile and beautiful paintings. They were important places for the people.

A mirror from the Kerma period.
Hans Ollermann, CC BY-SA 2.0 https://creativecommons.org/licenses/by-sa/2.0 via Wikimedia Commons; https://commons.wikimedia.org/wiki/File:Exposition_Nubia,_Land_of_the_Black_Pharaohs_%E2%80%93_Mirror,_Kerma_Period,_1700-1550_BC.jpg

Sadly, golden ages don't last forever. The people of Kerma had chosen not to move into the Upper Kingdom. Instead, they looted it and then left. The Egyptians who still lived there were loyal to the Egyptian king, not to the Kingdom of Kerma. This was Kerma's big mistake and its downfall.

In 1532 BCE, **Ahmose** (ah-mowz) sat on the throne of Egypt. He was determined to get his whole country back. He was an excellent military leader, and as **pharaoh** (Egypt's ruler), he led the army to defeat the Hyksos in 1530 BCE. Ahmose then turned his attention to Kerma.

Defeating Kerma was a difficult thing to do. They had the usual swords and spears, but their army specialized in **archery**. In ancient times, archers were feared because they could hit enemies at a distance. They could take down their enemy before they could come close enough to fight. The Kermaites were so good at archery that other armies would hire them to train their soldiers.

The Kermaites were also the first people in Africa to use war elephants. You may have heard of other armies using horses in battle, but the people of Africa didn't have horses yet. So, they trained elephants to carry heavy loads and fight in battle. Can you imagine trying to fight against an elephant? It would be really scary!

Ahmose knew that it would be a long fight with the Kingdom of Kerma. There were wins and losses on both sides. Finally, Egypt gained the upper hand under the leadership of **Pharaoh Thutmose** I. Kerma became part of Egypt, and that marked the end of the Kingdom of Kerma. Kerma and Egypt continued to trade and squabble throughout ancient African history because they both remembered being powerful civilizations.

Chapter 1 Activity Challenge

Can you fill in the blanks with the correct keyword?

| Sudan and Egypt | Classic Kerma | Hyksos | deffufa |
| Ancient Kerma | archery | Middle Kerma | Kerma |

1. The first capital city of the Kingdom of Kerma was called _____.

2. The kingdom was located in modern-day _____.

3. Kerma teamed up with the _____ to take over Egypt.

4. The _____ period lasted from 2500 BCE to 2050 BCE.

5. The Kermaites built _____ as special temples and for funeral services.

6. The _____ period lasted from 2050 BCE to 1750 BCE.

7. The army of Kerma specialized in _____.

8. The _____ period lasted from 1750 BCE to 1500 BCE and was the golden age of the kingdom.

Chapter 2: The Egyptian Kingdom

Ancient Egypt is one of the longest-lasting ancient civilizations. It existed from 3150 BCE to 30 BCE, when it was conquered by the Romans. But Egypt didn't stop existing under Roman rule. It continued on, and Egypt still exists today as a modern country. Their history is incredibly long and filled with mysterious pyramids, strong pharaohs, and inventions that would change the world.

There were people living in Egypt long before the first pharaoh took the throne. The **Nile** is the longest river in the world, and it flows from the middle of Africa to the **Mediterranean Sea**. This means it flows south to north. Living near the Nile was great for the ancient people. They had a reliable source of water and a way to transport people and goods. They farmed by digging irrigation ditches, and they were protected from invaders by the desert around them.

The people who settled around the Nile lived in two main areas. One group settled near the mountains in the south. They would eventually be called the **Upper Kingdom** because they were upriver. The other group settled down near the Mediterranean Sea. That group was called the **Lower Kingdom** because they were downriver. These two separate kingdoms were always fighting. They had a lot in common, like language and religion, but they didn't seem to like each other very much.

All of that changed when **King Menes I** took the throne in the Upper Kingdom around 3150 BCE. He was also called **King Narmer**. He fought with and conquered the Lower Kingdom, combining both kingdoms into one civilization. This started the **Early Dynastic period** of ancient Egyptian history.

Menes worked hard to convince the people of his new kingdom to get along. He moved the capital to the middle of the country to a city called **Memphis**. He even had a special crown made that had the main color of each kingdom on it to show his people the importance of being united.

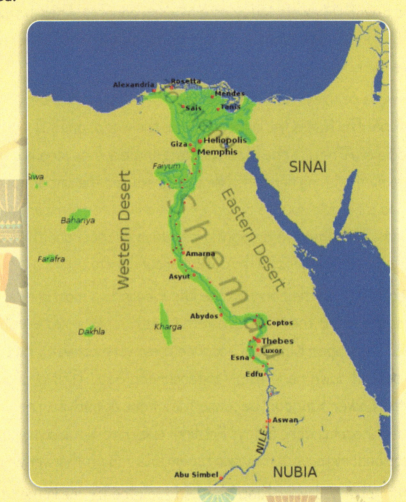

A map of ancient Egypt
Source: Vandal B~commonswiki Attribution-ShareAlike 3.0 Unported (CC BY-SA 3.0)
https://commons.wikimedia.org/wiki/File:Ancient_Egypt.png

The idea of having one ruler over all of Egypt became popular, especially because the people liked Menes. The next period of ancient Egyptian history is called the **Old Kingdom**. The Old Kingdom lasted from 2575 BCE until 2150 BCE. Even though Menes united the Upper and Lower Kingdoms, they didn't have an organized government until **Pharaoh Djoser** (jow-sr) came to the throne. He organized Egypt into **nomes** (districts), which helped solidify the government.

The Egyptians also used **hieroglyphics** to write official government documents. Hieroglyphics was the Egyptians' written language, and it was one of the first in the whole world. Although they were using hieroglyphics by 3100 BCE, Djoser made sure they were writing down important government things.

The Old Kingdom isn't really famous for its government reforms, though. The rulers of the Old Kingdom are famous for constructing the **pyramids**. In fact, this time is also called the **Age of the Pyramids**. You might recognize these structures. They are the most well-known structures in Egypt, and you can still see them today!

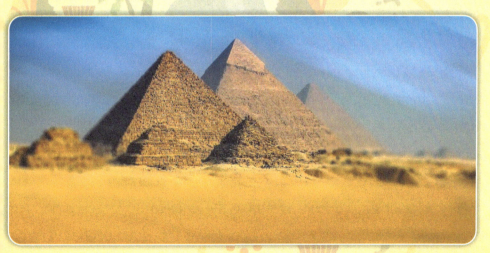

A picture of the pyramids of Giza.
Walkerssk, CC0, via Wikimedia Commons
https://commons.wikimedia.org/wiki/File:Pyramids_in_Giza_-_Egypt.jpg

The pyramids were built by the pharaohs as special tombs. They were large structures that showed off how wealthy the pharaohs were.

Pyramids were very expensive and very time-consuming to build. Most pharaohs started building their pyramids as soon as they took the throne.

Tombs were important to the Egyptians because they strongly believed in the afterlife. They believed that you had to bury yourself with everything you might need in your next life. They would fill their tombs with treasure and clay figurines. Sadly, other people wanted this treasure too, and most of the treasures that were buried in the pyramids were stolen by 1000 BCE.

But how did the Egyptians build these huge tombs? Archaeologists and historians don't fully know. They think that the pyramids were built by either slaves or local workers. There are ruined villages near the pyramids that show a community was established during the construction. It seems as if houses and food were provided for the workers and their families. Thousands of people had to work for many years to build each pyramid. There are about 138 pyramids in total.

The largest pyramid is called the **Great Pyramid of Giza**. Experts think it took twenty-three years to build and that over twenty thousand people worked on it. That's a lot of people! It took so long because every single stone had to be put in place by hand. The stones were really heavy, and they came from rock quarries along the Nile River. Historians still aren't sure how the ancient Egyptians managed it. Some of these rocks weighed about five thousand pounds. That's two and a half tons!

The ancient Egyptians even managed to build two different types of pyramids. One of the pyramids was flat and sloped on the outside. The other kind was called a **step pyramid**. They had things that looked like stairs on the outside. If the stones were small enough, you could climb all the way to the top.

The Pyramid of Djoser.
Gary Todd from Xinzheng, China, CC0, via Wikimedia Commons
https://commons.wikimedia.org/wiki/File:Saqqara_Step_Pyramid_of_Zoser_(Djoser)_(9794249344).jpg

Inside the pyramids were all kinds of rooms and burial chambers. Once the pharaoh died, he or she was turned into a **mummy**. Mummification was a special process that kept the body from decaying after death. The mummy would be placed in one of the burial rooms with all of the treasures that you could want in the afterlife. There were sometimes even fake burial chambers to confuse robbers.

The ancient Egyptians built many things during the Old Kingdom that we still have today. They built a lot of pyramids, and they also built the **Great Sphinx of Giza**. It has the body of a lion and the face of a man. The Egyptians built several different sphinx statues to guard places. The most famous one guards the pyramids at Giza.

The Great Sphinx of Giza is the oldest massive structure in Egypt! It was carved out of rock around 2500 BCE. The people in Egypt today work hard to keep the statue in good condition. They have to constantly repair it due to **erosion**, which is the weather trying to break down the statue and turn it into sand.

The Great Sphinx.
Nina R from Africa, CC BY 2.0 https://creativecommons.org/licenses/by/2.0 via Wikimedia Commons
https://commons.wikimedia.org/wiki/File:Giza_Pyramid_Complex_(39932845093).jpg

Even though the Old Kingdom produced some amazing buildings, it eventually fell. The **nomarchs** (nom-ahrks), or the governors of the nomes, became too powerful. They started to ignore the pharaoh and ran the nomes like private countries. The central government wasn't strong enough to stop them, and it collapsed. Egyptian history moved into the **First Intermittent Period**.

Although the people rallied back together during the **Middle Kingdom**, they were conquered by the Hyksos and the Kermaites during the **Second Intermittent Period**. The Egyptians were left with one major city, so the rightful rulers of Egypt had to huddle together there.

The Second Intermittent Period ended when Ahmose I became king. He was about ten years old when he came to the throne, but he would grow up to become a great ruler and military leader. Under his guidance, Egypt pushed the Hyksos out and became a unified country again. This started the **New Kingdom**. It lasted from 1520 BCE to 1075 BCE. The New Kingdom was the golden age of ancient Egyptian history.

During this time, Egypt conquered neighboring nations like Kush, Nubia, and Syria. They also got a lot of wealth from trading and from gold mines. The Egyptians used their new wealth to build temples. One of the most famous temples is the **Temple of Luxor**, which was built in Thebes.

The pharaohs also built special tombs for themselves, but they didn't use pyramids anymore. Instead, they built tombs in a place called the **Valley of the Kings**. Many pharaohs from the New Kingdom are buried here, and archaeologists have found all kinds of important things in these tombs like treasure and mummies.

Although the New Kingdom would eventually fall once Egypt began to interact with Rome, Egypt has remained one of the longest-lasting civilizations in the world. You can still visit it today to see the wonders that the ancient people left behind, which the people today still love and protect.

Chapter 2 Activity Challenge

If you thought this chapter was interesting, there's more to learn about ancient Egypt! Go to your local library or log onto your favorite history website to learn more about the ancient Egyptians. Make sure to always have a parent or guardian helping you with your research. Here are some topics to get you started!

- **Pharaoh Tutankhamun (King Tut)**
- **Moses and the ancient Israelites**
- **Cleopatra**
- **The Library of Alexandria**
- **The sun god Ra**
- **Hatshepsut (a female pharaoh!)**
- **Hieroglyphics**
- **Mummification**
- **Belief in the afterlife**
- **Children in ancient Egypt**
- **Pets in ancient Egypt**
- **The Rosetta Stone**

Chapter 3: The Kingdom of Kush

The **Kingdom of Kush** flowed with riches. Its people specialized in trading iron and gold. Both of those metals were precious in ancient times. Gold is still precious now! But living in a wealthy country didn't mean that things were always great in the kingdom.

A map of the Kingdom of Kush.
CristinaPalop, CC BY-SA 4.0 https://creativecommons.org/licenses/by-sa/4.0 via Wikimedia Commons
https://commons.wikimedia.org/wiki/File:Map_of_Kingdom_of_Kush.jpg

The Kingdom of Kush lasted from about 1069 BCE to 350 CE, but there were people in the area long before that. This part of Africa was called **Nubia**. Today, we call it **Sudan**. It is south of Egypt by the base of the Nile River and the base of the mountains. It was a good place to grow crops. Archaeologists believe that people were living in Nubia by 8000 BCE. In fact, the **Kingdom of Kerma** was in the same place! The Kushites shared some of their culture with the Kingdom of Kerma, but they also had things that made them special.

Kush first began to form after Kerma was defeated by the Egyptians around 1500 BCE. **Pharaoh Thutmose** III founded the city of **Napata** to make sure his control over the area was strong. Kush began as an Egyptian colony. It didn't stay a colony forever, though. Napata grew in wealth and power because it had close trade relations with Egypt. The Egyptians also built many temples in Napata, which increased the power of the city. The more temples a city had, the more powerful it was in ancient times.

A model of what the city of Kerma might have looked like. It is likely other large cities, like Napata, looked similar to this.
Matthias Gehricke, CC BY-SA 4.0 https://creativecommons.org/licenses/by-sa/4.0 via Wikimedia Commons
https://commons.wikimedia.org/wiki/File:Model_Kerma_capital.jpg

Eventually, the power of Egypt began to fail after the **New Kingdom** period. The people of Kush took advantage of that and began to exert their independence. Although Kush had existed as an Egyptian territory, the Kingdom of Kush officially began around 1069 BCE. That's when kings ruled Kush as a separate nation without Egypt interfering. Egypt was too busy dealing with its own problems to pay attention to the state just south of them.

The first capital of Kush was Napata. It would be the capital of the kingdom during the height of Kushite power. It was chosen because it had great access to trade routes. Even though Kush was now independent of Egypt, the two still traded with each other. Kush got much of its wealth from trading. Its two biggest resources were gold and iron. Iron was important because it could be used to make weapons. During the Iron Age, whoever had the best weapons tended to win, so everyone wanted the best iron weapons.

Gold was important because it was valuable. In fact, gold was so valuable that the Kushites set up the first **trans-Saharan trade route**. This trade route went over the **Sahara Desert**, which is the biggest desert in the world. Crossing the hot, sandy desert was really hard. It was dangerous because there wasn't a lot of food or water. But as long as the traders had their trusty camels, they could do it. The Kushites built their trade network all the way to West Africa.

The Kingdom of Kush grew richer and richer from trading. Eventually, it was so rich and powerful that it decided it would be easier to just take over Egypt than to continue to trade with them. So, around 746 BCE, **Kashta** declared himself king of Upper and Lower Egypt. He was already the king of Kush, but the Egyptians were so busy fighting each other that nobody challenged him.

In general, the royal Kushites loved Egyptian culture. In fact, the Kushites loved Egyptian culture so much that some historians believe the nobles thought they *were* Egyptians! The Kushites modeled their burial practices, religion, and government on Egypt. They built smaller pyramids as graves. They mummified their dead. They even worshiped the Egyptian gods, although they added a couple of their own gods to the group, like the three-headed lion god. While Kush ruled over Egypt, it continued to support the Egyptian culture. The Kushites even rebuilt some of the important Egyptian buildings.

The Kushites really loved Egypt, but they had some special things about them too. They were known as the **Land of the Bow**. They were really good archers, which was important in ancient times. Archers were range fighters. This means that they could attack an enemy before the enemy could attack them. Archers were important for winning battles.

Of course, the Kushites also had swords and the other usual weapons of war. They were reasonably good at fighting, and they put down several Egyptian rebellions during their rule of Egypt.

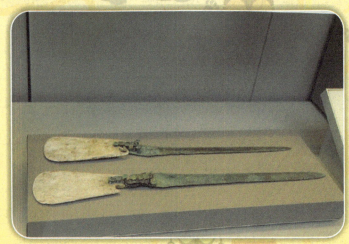

A picture of bronze swords from the Kingdom of Kush.
Gary Todd from Xinzheng, China, CC0, via Wikimedia Commons;
https://commons.wikimedia.org/wiki/File:Bronze_Swords_from_Kingdom_of_Kush_(35808393033).jpg

The Kushites did well in Egypt, but their time there was very short. **Shebitku** (sh-bit-ku) ruled from 707 to 690 BCE. That was during the time of the **Assyrians**. They were a powerful Mesopotamian civilization that was conquering pretty much everybody. It seemed as if no one stood a chance against the Assyrians. Shebitku tried to help some of the nations to the north of him fight the Assyrians. Once the Assyrians found out, they were angry. They came to Egypt and defeated the Kushites in 671 BCE. Luckily, **King Taharqa** (ta-har-ca) managed to escape to Napata. The Kushites continued to resist the Assyrians until they were completely defeated in 666 BCE.

This wasn't the end of the Kushites, though. They survived for over one thousand more years after the Assyrians conquered Egypt. They even built another great city called **Meroe** (mer-oh-ee). By about 590 BCE, Kush was getting tired of the Assyrian invasions. They moved their capital south to get away from them, and Meroe became the new capital of Kush.

The Kushites kept following Egyptian practices until **King Arkamani I**, who ruled from 295 to 275 BCE. He is also known as **Ergamenes** (erg-ah-means). He didn't like some of the Egyptian practices. He especially didn't like that the **priests of Amun** were so powerful that they decided when it was time for a king to die. As a new king, that could be scary! Arkamani killed all the priests and made the Kushite people abandon the Egyptian culture. They had to develop their own writing system as a result.

Part of the new culture was women leadership. After Arkamani I, women could be the rulers of Kush. Women were very important to the Kushite culture. The queens did not have to rely on men to give their titles any power. Instead, queens led the Kushite army into battle. **Queen Amanirenas** (a-mon-ur-renas) successfully fought off the Romans and negotiated a peace treaty between Kush and **Augustus Caesar**.

Some of the unique artifacts left behind by the Kushites.
Gary Todd from Xinzheng, China, CC0, via Wikimedia Commons
https://commons.wikimedia.org/wiki/File:Artifacts_from_Kingdom_of_Kush_(35808395143).jpg

The Kushites were a strong people who were good at war and trade. They loved Egyptian culture, but eventually, they developed their own. Kingdoms don't last forever, though. Kush was finally defeated by the **Kingdom of Aksum**. Meroe was in decline at this point. The people were running out of trees to burn for their ironwork, and their farming fields were not producing well. Aksum sacked Meroe around 330 CE. By 350 CE, Kush was another memory in the pages of history.

Chapter 3 Activity Challenge

Decide if the following statements about the Kingdom of Kush are true or false.

1. The Kingdom of Kush began around 1069 BCE.

2. Kerma, Napata, and Meroe were important Egyptian cities.

3. Kush did not have any queens.

4. Pharaoh Thutmose III founded Napata after Egypt defeated Kush around 1500 BCE.

5. Kush was famous for its silver and rubies.

6. Kush was also known as the Land of the Bow because the people were great archers.

7. The Assyrians defeated Kush and made them leave Egypt.

8. The trans-Saharan trade route was first set up by the Egyptians.

Chapter 4: Ancient Carthage

One of the greatest powers of the Mediterranean Sea came from the coast of Africa. We know that Egypt was a powerful country, but they didn't conquer the Mediterranean Sea like the city of **Carthage**. Carthage sits on the coast of North Africa. It is located in the modern country of Tunisia. Although the city does not exist anymore, you can still visit the ruins and imagine what it would have been like to live in Carthage. During the height of its power, it was stunning and wealthy!

The ruins of the Antonine Baths in Cartage.
Dennis Jarvis; author notes these are free to use; https://flic.kr/p/cXmS4G

But Carthage didn't start out that way. The city was founded in 814 BCE by the **Phoenician** (fuh-nee-shn) **Empire**. According to legend, it was founded by a queen. Her name was **Queen Elissa**, but she is also known as **Dido**. She was fleeing from her brother because he was a **tyrant** (a ruler more interested in power than their subjects' happiness). She landed on the coast of Africa.

The **Berber chieftain** who ruled that part of Africa allowed her to build a small city on a hill. He said he would give her as much land as an ox hide would cover. That's not a lot of land for a city! So, Dido had to get creative. She cut the ox hide up into thin strips. She then lined the strips up so that they completely circled the hill she wanted. The Berber chieftain let her have that hill, and she built Carthage.

The city started out as a small trading port. The Phoenicians used it to restock or repair their ships at first. Carthage won its independence from the Phoenicians in 650 BCE and kept growing. By the 4th century, Carthage was a major trading center and the most powerful city in the Mediterranean. The city controlled lots of lands that weren't directly connected to the city. It controlled most of the coast of Spain, the coast of North Africa, and several islands like Corsica, Sardinia, and Sicily.

Carthage got most of its wealth through trade. The rulers charged **tariffs** (special taxes) on the goods that were traded. Trade was so important to the city that it had a special harbor just for merchant boats. The harbor was huge and beautifully decorated with Greek sculptures. It had 220 docks, which means 220 boats could load or unload at the same time!

Carthage had a lot of merchant boats, but it also had a large **navy**. When you have that many valuable goods sailing around, you need to have boats that protect the merchant boats from pirates. The Carthaginian navy sailed all over the Mediterranean Sea to protect other Carthaginian boats and to keep money flowing into the city.

Of course, Carthage didn't only focus on trade. The people were also really good farmers, and they fought many wars with other cities. They conquered land around the Mediterranean Sea to increase trade, and they fought other cities for power and control of the area. The most famous wars that Carthage was involved in are called the **Punic Wars**. The Punic Wars were fought between Carthage and the **Roman Republic**, and they would eventually cause the end of ancient Carthage.

The **First Punic War** started in 264 BCE because Rome and Carthage fought each other over who got to control the island of **Sicily**. The island was divided into different groups called **factions**, and these groups didn't get along. Rome and Carthage supported a different faction, which led to war.

The First Punic War was fought between Rome's army and Carthage's navy. Rome didn't really have a navy at this point, although it worked on building one. Its first few ships were not successful. They were top-heavy and tended to flip over in the water. When you are trying to fight an enemy ship, you really don't want your boat to suddenly flip over.

The First Punic War lasted for twenty-five years. By 241 BCE, the Carthaginians were tired of fighting, so they asked for peace. The Romans celebrated their victory by taking control of all of Sicily and making Carthage pay a heavy fine.

After the First Punic War, Carthage needed more land to expand its trade. It had lost Sicily to the Romans, so it decided to conquer more land in Spain. Unfortunately, the Roman Republic got angry about this.

The Romans also had a few cities in Spain, and when **Hannibal Barca**, the general of the Carthaginian army, attacked one of those cities, Rome declared war. The Second Punic War started in 218 BCE.

The Romans controlled the sea, so Hannibal couldn't sneak back to Carthage. Spain and Italy are separated by the **Alps**, a steep and cold mountain range. Most people thought crossing the Alps was impossible. But Hannibal saw it as an opportunity. He marched his entire army over the Alps to attack Rome from the north. He even marched his thirty-seven war elephants over the mountains! Most of the war elephants did not survive the crossing because it was cold and dangerous. It is thought that only one made it across safely.

Once he was in Italy, Hannibal spent the next seventeen years fighting with the Romans. He didn't have a strong enough army to take the city of Rome, but he still won every major battle in Italy. The Roman army could not defeat Hannibal's unique and ingenious battle strategies. They were scrambling to find a way to stop him.

Finally, after huge losses, Roman General **Scipio Africanus** figured out the best way to get Hannibal out of Italy. He sent the Roman army to Carthage, and Carthage called Hannibal back home to help defend the city. This fight is called the **Battle of Zama**, and Rome eventually won.

The Second Punic War ended in 201 BCE. Carthage suffered because it had lost another war. It had to pay a huge fine to Rome, and it had to shrink its army. It also had to give more land to Rome. While Rome thought this was a good thing, Carthage was upset. It was having a hard time defending itself against other African cities and tribes.

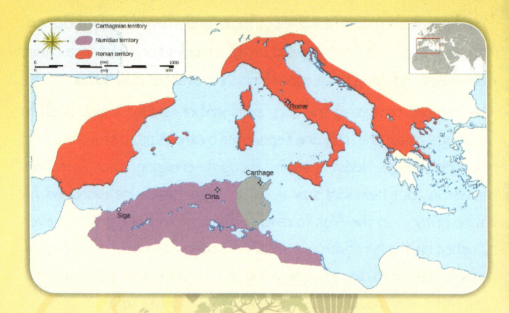

A map showing the three major powers of the western Mediterranean.
Goran tek-en, CC BY-SA 4.0 https://creativecommons.org/licenses/by-sa/4.0 via Wikimedia Commons
https://commons.wikimedia.org/wiki/File:Western_Mediterranean_territory,_150_BC.svg

By 149 BCE, Rome decided that it wanted to completely destroy Carthage. The Romans didn't like that there was another powerful city on the Mediterranean Sea. They ordered Carthage to dismantle its army and move the city inland. Carthage would be vulnerable to attacks without an army, and moving the city inland would strip away its trading power. Carthage said no.

Rome didn't care that its demands were unreasonable. The Romans declared war on Carthage in 149 BCE and immediately sailed to the city. This war is called the **Third Punic War**. The Romans **besieged** Carthage for three years. Sieging a city is a classic military tactic. An army camps around the city it wants to conquer and makes sure that no one goes in or out. This means that no food or water can go into the city. If the siege is not broken, the city eventually has to surrender so that they can get more food and water.

It took Carthage three years to surrender. When it did, the Roman army destroyed the city. They burned the city down to make sure that no one could live there anymore. They also sold all the survivors into slavery. Today, we know that this is wrong, but back then, selling defeated enemies into slavery was a normal practice.

What Carthage looks like today.
https://commons.wikimedia.org/wiki/File:Tunis_Carthage_Odeon_2.jpg

Carthage was a great African city. It controlled the trade in the Mediterranean Sea for many years, but Rome eventually became more powerful. When Carthage finally fell in 146 BCE, all of its lands became part of the Roman Republic. Rome grew more powerful, building its empire in North Africa on Carthage's foundations.

Chapter 4 Activity Challenge

Can you match the historical events with the correct dates?

| 201 BCE | 146 BCE | 264 BCE |
| 218 BCE | 814 BCE | 650 BCE |

1. The year Carthage was first established.

2. The First Punic War started in this year.

3. Carthage was destroyed by the Romans during this year.

4. The year that Carthage won its independence from the Phoenicians.

5. Rome began the Second Punic War with Carthage in this year.

6. The Battle of Zama ended the Second Punic War in this year.

Chapter 5: Roman North Africa/Africa Proconsularis

After Rome sacked Carthage, it took over all the land that had belonged to Carthage. That meant that Rome took over part of the African coastline, which is how Roman power first came to Africa. This area of the empire was called **Africa Proconsularis** (pro-kon-su-la-ris), but it is also called **Roman North Africa**. It was focused around where Carthage had been, but it soon expanded westward toward the modern-day Algerian-Tunisian border. It also expanded eastward and southward. In all, Roman North Africa had lands in modern-day Algeria, Tunisia, and Libya.

A map of Roman North Africa.

Milenioscuro, CC BY-SA 4.0 https://creativecommons.org/licenses/by-sa/4.0 via Wikimedia Commons
https://commons.wikimedia.org/wiki/File:Roman_Empire_-_Africa_Proconsularis_(125_AD).svg

Africa Proconsularis was established in 146 BCE, right after the fall of Carthage. Rome completely destroyed the city, but the land was still good. Some historians believe that when Rome destroyed Carthage, it also sowed salt into the farmland. That might seem strange to us, but if the ground is really salty, plants have a hard time growing. That would make the land bad for farming and keep anyone from trying to live there. Other historians don't think the Romans salted the farmland because as soon as Carthage was destroyed, Rome took over all of that land. The Romans took the best farmland, and they quickly began to grow food. So, it is unlikely that the Romans salted the Carthaginian land, which they used to grow food for their growing empire.

In 122 BCE, **Gaius Sempronius Gracchus** (guy-us sim-pro-ne-us grac-cus) tried to found a colony on the coast of Africa. It was not successful, but many Roman farmers and traders saw an opportunity. They moved to Africa Proconsularis and began working to improve their lives. Rome continued to try to colonize the coast of Africa. By the 1st century BCE, they were successful. **Julius Caesar** started colonizing in 46 BCE, but his plans were finished by **Augustus**.

As the Romans colonized Africa Proconsularis, they had to deal with the **indigenous people** (the people who were already living there). The largest group the Romans dealt with was called the **Berbers**. Historians believe that when the Romans took over the northern coast of Africa, there were several different tribes living there. They had similar customs and traditions, but they weren't the same groups of people. The Romans didn't specify, though. Instead, they called all the indigenous people "Berber," which comes from the Roman word "barbarian." Although we might think "barbarian" is a rude word, the Romans used it to mean anyone who was not Roman.

The Berbers were not strong enough to fight off the Romans, but they were strong enough to survive the Roman invasion. The Roman invasion wasn't the first invasion they had faced. The Berbers had lived in Africa for thousands of years. During ancient times, the different tribes were never able to unite as one group. That meant they were vulnerable to invasions. Other nations set up colonies on their land. All these other people groups influenced the Berbers, changing their culture little by little.

The Berbers didn't keep their own written records, so historians have to trace their history through other records. The ancient Egyptians were the first people to mention the Berbers. They are first mentioned during the Egyptian **Predynastic period**, which lasted from 6000 BCE to 3150 BCE. Both the Greeks and the Romans have records about the Berbers. After Rome fell, the Berber people continued on. They met other groups of people, like the Arabs.

Berber red slip flagons and vases, 2nd–4th centuries.
AgTigress, CC BY-SA 3.0 https://creativecommons.org/licenses/by-sa/3.0 via Wikimedia Commons
https://commons.wikimedia.org/wiki/File:African_Red_Slip_vessels.JPG

The Berbers are still on the coast of North Africa today. They speak their own language and have their own traditions, like special music and dances. Some Berbers are nomadic and live in tents as they travel with their herds of animals, but most of them are farmers.

The Romans used the Berbers' talent as farmers to help the Roman Empire grow. For a long time, Africa Proconsularis helped produce a lot of food for the Romans. The area was so important that the Romans did a lot of urbanization. **Urbanization** is when people build up a city in a certain area. You might see this happening today. Have you ever noticed a new shopping center where fields used to be? The Romans weren't focused on building malls, though. They were focused on building **temples** and **amphitheaters**.

Temple of August Piety in Dougga, an ancient Roman city in what is now Tunisia.
Dennis Jarvis; author notes these are free to use; https://flic.kr/p/cXfYuJ

The Romans rebuilt Carthage as a Roman city. It eventually became the second most powerful city in the empire. There were also many **estates** in the area, which were lands owned by individuals. For several centuries, Roman North Africa did well under Roman rule. It was wealthy. There was a lot of trade. They sold olives, grains, and animal hides. There were also several art schools. There were schools for **sculpting** and schools for **mosaics**. Can you imagine living in such a busy and wealthy area? There would have been so much to learn and do!

The amphitheater in Thysdrus.
User Andyavery on en.wikipedia, CC BY-SA 3.0 http://creativecommons.org/licenses/by-sa/3.0/ via Wikimedia Commons https://commons.wikimedia.org/wiki/File:Eljem2.jpg

Even though the area did well while the Romans lived there, Africa Proconsularis eventually started to fade. By the end of the 300s

CE, Africa Proconsularis was not as strong as it used to be. In 430, the **Vandals** reached the coast of Africa. The Vandals were a Germanic tribe. Rome had fought them for years in Europe. As the Roman Empire weakened, the Vandals won more fights. They fought their way into Italy and into Rome itself. It was a huge blow to the Romans. The Vandals began moving all over the Roman Empire, looking for food and money. When they landed on the northern coast of Africa, they made Carthage their new capital.

As the Roman Empire fell apart, the eastern half of the empire grew strong. This empire became known as the **Byzantine Empire**. It had some of the same interests as Rome, but it was not really involved in what was going on in the western half of Europe. The Byzantine Empire did kick the Vandals out of Carthage in 533 CE, but Africa Proconsularis was too weak to defend itself. The mighty Roman Empire was now gone. In 698, Africa Proconsularis gave in to the Arab invaders without much of a fight. Their time as a Roman territory was officially over.

Roman North Africa was an important part of African history. The northern coast was essential to the Roman Empire because it had good farmland. The Romans built cities and let people become Roman citizens. During ancient times, that was a really big deal. For a long time, the area thrived, and you can still visit the ruins today and imagine what living in the second-most important Roman city might have been like.

Chapter 5 Activity Challenge

Can you define or describe the following terms?

1. Indigenous

2. Urbanization

3. The Byzantine Empire

4. Barbarian

5. Africa Proconsularis

6. The Vandals

Chapter 6: The Kingdom of Aksum

The **Kingdom of Aksum** was one of the most advanced ancient African civilizations. This kingdom is sometimes called **ancient Ethiopia**. The Kingdom of Aksum had its own coins and written language. During ancient times, this was a really big deal! It shows how advanced they were as a civilization.

Ancient Ethiopia was located on the southern coast of the Red Sea. It covered a big piece of land. The kingdom covered modern-day Ethiopia, Eritrea, Saudi Arabia, and Somalia. The Kingdom of Aksum ruled this area of Africa from about 100 BCE to 960 CE. That's over one thousand years!

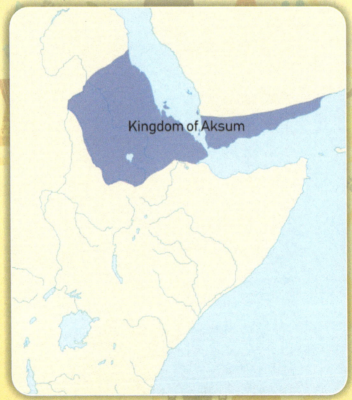

A map of the Kingdom of Aksum.
Aldan-2, CC BY-SA 4.0 https://creativecommons.org/licenses/by-sa/4.0 via Wikimedia Commons; https://commons.wikimedia.org/wiki/File:The_Kingdom_of_Aksum.png

There's a legend that says the Kingdom of Aksum is even older. According to legend, the Kingdom of Aksum was founded in 400 BCE by the son of **King Solomon** and the **Queen of Sheba**. King Solomon was a king of ancient Israel, and he was famous for being wise. He was so famous that many other civilizations knew about his wisdom. According to the story told in the Bible, the Queen of Sheba traveled to Israel to talk to Solomon. She was amazed at his wisdom. The Bible story does not mention them having a child. Ancient Ethiopian legend says that they had a son, and he eventually founded the Kingdom of Aksum.

Historians have not been able to prove this story, but they do know that there were people living in that area of Africa long before the Kingdom of Aksum began. Archaeologists believe there were farming communities in this area during the **Stone Age**. The Kingdom of Aksum did not prosper until around 100 BCE. It had rich farming lands, which helped the people become wealthy. They could grow all kinds of grain, like wheat and barley. They also had all kinds of animals, like cows and goats. All of this food made Aksum wealthy.

They were also located in a good spot for trade. Trade is all about being in the right place at the right time. And Aksum was certainly in the right place! They linked Egypt to the eastern coast of Africa and Arabia to the western trading cities. All of this wealth gave the Kingdom of Aksum more power, and it consolidated into a cohesive civilization in the late 1st century CE.

The kingdom grew slowly until **King Ezana I** came to the throne. He ruled from 325 to 360 CE, and he was focused on making the Kingdom of Aksum bigger. He wanted his kingdom to conquer more land

and become a powerful and important trading center. As the kingdom grew, merchants came from all over the world. They even came from as far away as Rome and the Byzantine Empire to trade at Aksum.

You could find all kinds of things at Aksum. Traders sold gold, salt, precious gems, iron, bronze lamps, olive oil, and wine. Can you imagine what walking through the marketplace would have been like? People spoke Greek to trade, but there still would have been many different languages and so many things to look at. During the height of its power, Aksum was a busy place!

To help make trade easier, Aksum became the first sub-Saharan civilization to make its own coins. It made coins out of gold, silver, and bronze. The coins usually had a picture on them, like a portrait of a king. We know Aksum traded with a lot of different people because their coins have been found in many different countries.

Silver coin of Ezana.
https://commons.wikimedia.org/wiki/File:Ezana.jpg

But the Kingdom of Aksum wasn't only focused on trade. Under King Ezana I, they worked on expanding their land. Aksum conquered the nations and tribes around it, but it didn't rule over them. Instead of replacing their government, the conquered tribes were allowed to rule themselves. They just had to pay **tribute**, which is similar to a tax. They had to pay Aksum hundreds of cattle. We might think that's a weird tax today, but cattle were very valuable back then. In some parts of Africa today, cattle are still very valuable!

King Ezana I fought with the **Kingdom of Kush**. The two kingdoms fought over the ivory trade. **Ivory** comes from elephant tusks, and it is still valuable today. Both kingdoms wanted to control the ivory trade because they wanted to make more money.

Historians are still figuring out who started the war. The written records are not clear. We do know that King Ezana I responded to the conflict by sending a big army to **Meroe**, the capital of Kush. The Kingdom of Aksum destroyed the city and ended the Kingdom of Kush. When Kush fell, Aksum didn't have any other strong enemies. It took control of the whole region.

This made them very wealthy. They spent some of their money on building up their capital. The capital of the Kingdom of Aksum was **Aksum**, but it is sometimes also called **Axum**. To separate the kingdom from the city, we will call the city Axum. Axum started in the 1st century CE, and it's still an active city today. You can visit it in northern Ethiopia. It's a small city now, but Axum is one of the oldest continually occupied cities in Africa.

When Axum was the capital of the Kingdom of Aksum, it was a really important trading center. It also had a lot of ceremonial buildings. The most famous ceremonial structures are the **stelae** (stuh-lay). Stelae were tall towers. Most of them were around seventy-eight feet tall, but the tallest one was about one hundred feet tall. They were usually decorated. They had carvings, stone doors, and fake windows. Most of the stelae were used as tomb markers. They were an important addition to the ceremonial monuments in the capital.

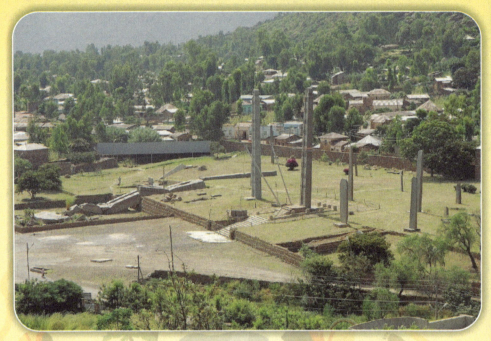

Stelae Park in Axum.
JensiS65, CC BY-SA 3.0 https://creativecommons.org/licenses/by-sa/3.0 via Wikimedia Commons; https://commons.wikimedia.org/wiki/File:Stelenpark_in_Axum_2010.JPG

There were other large buildings in Axum that were probably used by royalty. The large buildings were built with stepped foundations. The

Ruins of Dungur in Aksum.
A.Savin (WikiCommons), FAL, via Wikimedia Commons
https://commons.wikimedia.org/wiki/File:ET_Axum_asv2018-01_img48_Dungur.jpg

rocks were decorated, and there was a special staircase that led to the entrance of the building itself. Some of the buildings had basements and water cisterns inside. For that time in history, having water inside the building was impressive.

The Kingdom of Aksum continued to expand, taking over parts of southern Arabia, which was across the Red Sea. Aksum eventually declined in power. It had to fight rebellions with the tribes it had already conquered. It also had to fight other people who were moving into the area, especially the Islamic people. By the end of the 8th century CE, the Kingdom of Aksum's power was fading, leaving room for another great African civilization to rise.

Chapter 6 Activity Challenge

Can you select the correct answer for these multiple-choice questions?

1. What is another name for the Kingdom of Aksum?

    a) Egypt　　　　　　　　　b) Ancient Ethiopia

    c) Wagadu　　　　　　　　d) Arabia

2. According to legend, who first established Aksum?

    a) The son of King Solomon　　b) An Egyptian pharaoh

    c) Hannibal Barca　　　　　　d) Julius Caesar

3. When did the Kingdom of Aksum first rise to power?

    a) 500 CE　　　　　　　　b) 200 BCE

    c) 400 BCE　　　　　　　 d) 350 CE

4. What are the tall ceremonial towers in Axum called?

    a) Obelisks　　　　　　　　b) Towers

    c) Stelae　　　　　　　　　d) Guardhouses

5. Which of these places did the Kingdom of Aksum NOT trade with?

    a) Rome　　　　　　　　　b) Arabia

    c) Great Britain　　　　　　d) Egypt

Chapter 7: The Empire of Ancient Ghana

The **Empire of Ancient Ghana** (or the Ghana Empire) was another powerful African civilization. It also acquired most of its wealth and power through trade. Ancient Ghana was not in the same place that the **Republic of Ghana** is today. Ancient Ghana was located on the west side of Africa. There were several rivers in the empire, like the **Niger River** and the **Gambia River**. Rivers provided fresh drinking water and food, and they also worked like highways. People would take their boats up and down the rivers with things to trade. Although roads weren't reliable back then, the rivers were. Because ancient Ghana had so many great rivers, it became a very important trading center for Africa.

Map of the Ghana Empire.
Luxo, CC BY-SA 3.0 http://creativecommons.org/licenses/by-sa/3.0/
via Wikimedia Commons; https://commons.wikimedia.org/wiki/File:Ghana_empire_map.png

Ancient Ghana started in 300 CE, and it lasted until about 1200 CE. We don't know a lot about the early years of ancient Ghana because there is almost no historical information. We do know that the Empire of Ancient Ghana had a king. The king ruled over lots of other smaller tribes. These tribes all had their own leaders, and those leaders all listened to the king. The first king of Ghana was **King Dinga Cisse** (ding-a sis-sa). He came from the **Soninke** (son-ing-cow) **people**, and he brought all the tribes in the area together to form Ghana.

Did you know that this empire had two names? People who didn't live in this area called it Ghana, but the people inside the empire did not. "Ghana" was their word for "king," although it can also be translated as "warrior king." The people who lived in the empire called it **Wagadu** (wa-ga-du).

We don't know much about the early years of Ghana. This isn't a lot of writing from back then. Without written records, historians don't have enough information to get a clear picture of what life was like back then. The first time Ghana was mentioned in writing was during the 700s CE. Ghana had become an important empire by then.

It got most of its power and wealth from trading. Ancient Ghana wanted to get involved with the gold trade because gold was valuable, so it became part of the **trans-Saharan trade route.** They were in the perfect spot for traders to exchange precious items like gold, salt, and iron. Can you believe the ancient people treated salt like it was a valuable thing? We might be surprised because salt is cheap today, but back then, salt was important for survival. Salt helped people preserve food. Your body also needs a certain amount of salt every day. If you don't eat enough salt, you can get really sick. Our food today usually has enough salt, but the ancient people knew how important salt was for their survival.

The people of ancient Ghana didn't only trade with the countries around them. As part of the trans-Saharan trade route, they also traded with the **Middle East**, even though that trip could take forty days. Can you imagine riding a camel across a desert for forty days? That's over a month! Because Ghana traded a lot, it became very wealthy. It charged a tax on everything that came into and left the empire. If goods were coming in, Ghana charged an **import tax**. If goods were leaving, Ghana charged an **export tax**. When you are taxing gold and other precious materials, those taxes can make you wealthy quickly!

Chinguetti is located in today's Mauritania.
François COLIN, CC BY-SA 2.5 https://creativecommons.org/licenses/by-sa/2.5 via Wikimedia Commons; https://commons.wikimedia.org/wiki/File:Chinguetti-Vue_Goblale_Vieille_ville.jpg

The capital of Ghana became a very important trading center. People came from as far as the Middle East to trade in Ghana. The capital moved a few times during the empire's history. One of the more well-known capitals was **Koumbi Saleh** (com-bi sal-eh). This was the capital during the 11th century CE. Koumbi Saleh was a big city. Archaeologists think that up to twenty thousand people lived in and around Koumbi Saleh.

Ancient Ghana was such a strong trade center because it also had a strong army. It had an army of 200,000 soldiers. The Ghana Empire used its large army to protect its trade routes. Traders were always in danger of robbers in ancient times. Robbers wanted to steal gold and salt, and they weren't afraid to use violence to get what they wanted. Ancient Ghana didn't want to lose its gold, salt, or traders, so it used its big army to protect the traders and their cargo.

Koumbi Saleh, Mauritania.
Eric Gaba (Sting - fr:Sting), CC BY-SA 3.0 https://creativecommons.org/licenses/by-sa/3.0 via Wikimedia Commons; https://commons.wikimedia.org/wiki/File:Mauritania_location_map.svg

Ghana also used its army to conquer territories. It took over smaller nations and lands, especially places that produced gold. The richer Ghana became, the more land it conquered. This made it an even more powerful trading empire.

Around 1050 CE, some of the **Muslim** tribes from the north began pressuring Ghana to convert to Islam. They called it a **holy war**. In general, a holy war is when a religious group fights another group or country. They usually say it's about converting people to their religion. Sometimes, it is. Other times, the religious group uses their religion as a disguise to try to get money or power. Many religious groups have fought in holy wars throughout history, and there are almost always multiple reasons for the wars.

The kings of Ghana did not want to fight a holy war. They wanted to continue trading so they could make more money. When they refused to convert to Islam, the Muslim tribes attacked. They didn't hold power over Ghana for long, but their attack weakened the empire's trade. Ghana needed its trade routes to be protected, but it had to spend many years fighting off attacks from these Muslim tribes. All of this fighting made traders feel unsafe traveling to Ghana. Without their trade, the Ghana Empire grew weaker.

Eventually, the lands that Ghana had conquered began to break away. The empire was too weak to stop them. Without land and money, what was left of the great Empire of Ancient Ghana was eventually absorbed by the **Mali Empire**. This ended the influence of this great African trading center.

Chapter 7 Activity Challenge

Can you match the term with the right fact?

1. Wagadu
2. King Dinga Cisse
3. Trans-Saharan trade route
4. Gold and salt
5. Ghana
6. Mali Empire
7. Koumbi Saleh

a. The most well-known capital of the Ghana Empire.

b. The king from the Soninke people who united ancient Ghana.

c. The forty-day journey across the Sahara Desert.

d. The nation that eventually conquered Ghana.

e. Literally translates as "Warrior King."

f. The name that the people used to refer to the empire.

g. Two very valuable items that ancient Ghana traded.

Chapter 8: Society and Famous Rulers

Ancient Africa was full of advanced societies. The civilizations in this book had class structures and important leaders. They had strong militaries and artists. The civilizations in ancient Africa were important to the ancient world, and they were powerful enough to change world history. Let's look at their societies and learn more about some of their famous rulers.

Egypt

Ancient Egypt was a very wealthy nation. It had social classes, like slaves and the pharaohs, but most people were farmers. They used the Nile to get most of their water because Egypt is really hot and dry. The people didn't get to keep the grain they grew. Instead, it was all stored in royal granaries. Can you imagine how it might feel to put in all the work of growing your own food without even getting to keep it?

The government was mostly ruled by the pharaoh, but the pharaoh had lots of help running the government. There were people like the **vizier** (vi-zeer), who was the chief overseer of Egypt, and the **nomarchs**, who were like governors. The ordinary people didn't have any say in their government, but they thought the pharaoh was a god. They didn't have a problem with a god ruling their country.

Pharaoh Menes I

Pharaoh Menes I is legendary. There are historical tablets that have his name on them, but some historians think that "Menes" is a title, not a name. So, some historians don't think Pharaoh Menes I even existed, even though he is supposed to be the first pharaoh of Egypt. They think the first pharaoh of Egypt was named Narmer. Sometimes, the names are used interchangeably.

If Pharoah Menes I existed, he ruled Egypt around 3150 BCE. He is famous for uniting the two halves of Egypt. At the beginning of Egyptian history, the Upper Kingdom and the Lower Kingdom were separate. After Menes became the ruler of the Upper Kingdom, he marched his army up the Nile River to the Lower Kingdom (remember, the Nile flows south to north). Then, Menes conquered the Lower Kingdom and united Egypt into one nation.

The cartouche (an image of a name) of Menes on the Abydos King List.
Abydos_Königsliste_06.jpg: Olaf Tauschderivative work: JMCC1, CC BY 3.0
https://creativecommons.org/licenses/by/3.0 via Wikimedia Commons
https://commons.wikimedia.org/wiki/File:Abydos_KL_01-01_n01.jpg

Kush

The Kushites loved Egyptian culture, so they modeled their society after Egypt. They had a king and powerful priests who had some say in the government. Most of the people were farmers, and they grew wheat, barley, and cotton. Some people traded things like gold and iron. This brought a lot of wealth to Kush, which allowed them to build things like pyramids.

But Kush also had parts of society that were unique. The Kushites were known for their military. Kush was known as **the Land of the Bow** because it was home to many great archers. Their archers were famous. Good archers were an important part of the ancient military, and Kush made sure that its archers were trained to be helpful during battles. Kush appreciated its archers so much that it even included them in their ancient artwork.

Rulers of Kush.
Matthias Gehricke, CC BY-SA 4.0 https://creativecommons.org/licenses/by-sa/4.0 via Wikimedia Commons; https://commons.wikimedia.org/wiki/File:Rulers_of_Kush,_Kerma_Museum.jpg

Pharaoh Piye

Piye (pi) was the king of Kush from around 750 BCE to 719 BCE. He is most famous for conquering Egypt. Kush was located south of Egypt, so it was easy for King Piye to march his army there. Egypt was very weak at this time in history, so it wasn't able to stop Piye. He started by taking over Upper Egypt and conquering the capital of **Memphis**. Then, King Piye marched into Lower Egypt. Many of the Egyptian leaders submitted to his rule, including the last pharaoh of the **23rd Dynasty**. That made Piye the next pharaoh of Egypt. Once he was the ruler of Egypt, Pharaoh Piye returned home to Kush to celebrate his victory. He is remembered in Egyptian history for conquering the nation and helping to start the **25th Dynasty**.

Piye's pyramid at El-Kurru.
Bertramz, CC BY 3.0 https://creativecommons.org/licenses/by/3.0 via Wikimedia Commons; https://commons.wikimedia.org/wiki/File:Al-Kurru,main_pyramid.jpg

Carthage

Carthage was a very powerful empire around the Mediterranean Sea. It got most of its money and power from trade. Only the wealthy and the ruling class could afford to live in houses in the city. The poor people lived outside the city in huts or apartments.

Carthage's government changed during its history. It started as a monarchy. Everyone listened to the king. In the 4th century BCE, the government changed to a republic. Carthage now had a senate that made the laws. The senate was made up of three hundred wealthy men. Carthage also elected two leaders every year called **suffetes** (su-feets) to help lead the empire.

Hannibal Barca

Hannibal was one of the greatest generals in history. He was one of the generals for Carthage during the **Second and Third Punic Wars**. Rome was fighting with Carthage, and Hannibal decided to attack Rome from a direction they didn't expect. Italy has the **Alps** on its northern border. Mountains are a good natural defense system because they are hard to get over. Hannibal didn't let the mountains scare him away. Instead, he marched his army over the Alps and into Italy. He even tried to take his war elephants over the mountains!

Hannibal then spent the next fifteen years in Italy fighting the Romans. He won many battles, even though he had fewer soldiers. This was because he managed to outsmart the Romans. They were scared of what Hannibal might do, but he never took Rome.

Hannibal and the Romans reached a **stalemate**, which is when neither side is really the winner. Hannibal eventually had to go back to Carthage. Ultimately, Rome won the Second Punic War, as well as the Third Punic War.

General Hannibal.
https://commons.wikimedia.org/wiki/File:Mommsen_p265.jpg

Aksum

Aksum got most of its wealth from trade, but it did have a strong military and lots of farmers. Aksum had lots of hills, so the people used **terrace farming** to grow more crops. Terrace farming is when people make large flat surfaces on the side of hills. The flat surfaces look like giant stairs when it's done. It helps people grow more food.

The society of Aksum was very advanced. The people had a written language. They also made their own coins. Instead of just trading and bartering, they used money to pay for things, just like we do. After the 4th century, Christianity became an important part of their society because King Ezana converted to that religion. The people built lots of churches, but it took a couple of centuries for the temples to close down in some of the cities.

King Ezana

King Ezana was the king who helped Aksum defeat **Kush**. He ruled Aksum from about 325 to 360 CE. To help his country grow stronger, he conquered the nearby lands. Kush was close by, and it wasn't the big and powerful country it used to be. King Ezana destroyed its capital, **Meroe**, and took the land for his own kingdom. Aksum was now free to grow and become a strong nation built on trade, and it was all thanks to King Ezana's hard work.

Ancient Ghana

Ancient Ghana was famous for its trade and ironworkers, but most of the people who lived in Ghana were farmers. The local leader gave everyone a piece of land to grow crops on. The farmers didn't even own their land! Despite that, they still lived good lives. The people were safe and had plenty to eat.

The Ghana Empire was a **monarchy**. This means the king was in charge. But the king usually let the local tribal leaders run their tribes. They still had to obey the king, but they also still had some power. When the king died, the next king was his sister's son. This is a little different than other kingdoms, but it certainly worked well for the Ghana Empire.

King Dinga Cisse

Dinga Cisse was the first king of Ghana. Before him, Ghana wasn't really a kingdom at all. Instead, the area was home to several different tribes. Although they sometimes worked together, they were still different groups.

That all changed with Dinga Cisse. He came from the Soninke people, and he united the tribes in the area under one ruler. Because he united the tribes, he was the first ruler. The Soninke people were very important in the government because they were King Dinga Cisse's people.

Chapter 8 Activity Challenge

Can you match the leader with their civilization?

1. Hannibal Barca
2. Pharaoh Piye
3. King Dinga Cisse
4. Pharaoh Menes I
5. King Ezana

a. Egypt
b. Ancient Ghana
c. Carthage
d. Kush
e. Aksum

Chapter 9: Culture and Art

The civilizations in ancient Africa were more than just important trading posts. They were important societies that had culture and art.

One of the most important parts of any civilization is its **written language.** In fact, historians say that a written language is essential to a group of people actually being a civilization. Writing is important to understand history. We can learn a lot about people by what they write down. We learn more from what they write down than from the things they leave behind, like tools or houses. But every civilization has its own language, which means they write things down differently.

Ancient Egypt used a writing style called **hieroglyphics**. They used pictures to represent letters or even whole words. You could write your hieroglyphics in any way you wanted to. You could write it upside down or right to left. It makes it a little confusing to translate today. The ancient Egyptians also used **Hieratic** (hahy-uh-rat-ik) and **Demotic** (dih-mot-ik) writing systems. Hieratic was like hieroglyphics, but it was simpler and had fewer symbols. Demotic has no symbols at all, and it looks more like other ancient writing systems.

Kush used a lot of different writing systems, including the same writing systems that the Egyptians used. They also wrote in Old Nubian and in **Meroitic** (meh-row-i-tuhk). Meroitic was invented in the 1st century BCE. **King Arkamani I** wanted to move away from Egyptian culture, so he made the people of Kush get rid of everything Egyptian, including hieroglyphics. Historians aren't able to translate Meroitic, though! They are still working on learning the language. Until then, they don't know what the Kushite documents written in Meroitic say.

Because of the Roman influence, a lot of North African civilizations wrote in Latin. Aksum invented a writing system called **Ge'ez** (gee-ez). It had letters for vowels and consonants, but their letters look very different from letters in the English language. Ge'ez became popular in Aksum as a written language, and it is still used today in Ethiopia.

Did you know that civilizations can use multiple languages? Aksum was such a big trading center in the ancient world that it didn't only use its language. The people wrote a lot of things down in Ge'ez, but they used ancient Greek as a commonly spoken language. It made it easier to trade in the market because everyone could understand each other.

Of course, writing isn't the only part of a culture. **Architecture** is also really important. Architecture is the art of making buildings and monuments. Historians and archaeologists usually focus on really important buildings because they were built for a special reason.

Both ancient Egypt and Kush built pyramids. Ancient Egypt built its pyramids during the **Old Kingdom**, and they were built as burial places for the pharaohs. Some of the Egyptian pyramids have steps, like the **Step Pyramid of Djoser at Saqqara** (suh-kahr-uh). It was built around 2630 BCE. It's over four thousand years old!

Other pyramids in Egypt have smooth sides. The most famous smooth pyramids are the **pyramids of Giza**. There are several pyramids close together in Giza, and they were built out of blocks of limestone. Historians don't know how the Egyptians moved the limestone and stacked it perfectly, but you can still see the pyramids in Egypt today.

The pyramids of Giza.
Ricardo Liberato, CC BY-SA 2.0 https://creativecommons.org/licenses/by-sa/2.0
via Wikimedia Commons; https://commons.wikimedia.org/wiki/File:All_Gizah_Pyramids.jpg

Ancient Egypt wasn't the only civilization to build pyramids. The Kushites loved Egyptian culture so much that they also built pyramids.

Nubian pyramids.
https://commons.wikimedia.org/wiki/File:Nubia_pyramids1.JPG

They used their pyramids as burial tombs as well. Kushite leaders were even turned into mummies after they died. Their pyramid would be filled with treasures to help them in the next life. Kushite pyramids were usually smaller than Egyptian pyramids, and you can still see them today.

Unlike Egypt and Kush, Aksum did not build pyramids. They are most famous for tall towers called **stelae**. The tallest stela was about 108 feet tall, but most of them were about 78 feet tall. The stelae were ceremonial. They were usually grave markers, and they were decorated with doors and fake windows.

The people of Aksum also built their stone palaces and other buildings without **mortar**. Mortar is the mixture that holds bricks and stones together like glue. Instead of mortar, the people made sure the stones fit together very tightly. They would decorate their stone buildings with clay.

Dry-laid stone structure in Sukur, Nigeria.
SULE, CC BY-SA 4.0 https://creativecommons.org/licenses/by-sa/4.0
via Wikimedia Commons; https://commons.wikimedia.org/wiki/File:Sukur-8.jpg

After the 4th century CE, Aksum began building churches. Christianity was popular in the kingdom, so they devoted energy to making churches. The old temples were still open into the 6th century CE, so for a while, the two religions coexisted.

The ruins of a temple at Yeha, Ethiopia.
Jialiang Gao www.peace-on-earth.org CC BY-SA 3.0
http://creativecommons.org/licenses/by-sa/3.0/ via Wikimedia Commons
https://commons.wikimedia.org/wiki/File:Yeha_Tigray_Ethiopia.jpg

Architecture is a way for cultures to express themselves, but there are other ways to do this. Historians can learn a lot about ancient civilizations by studying their art. They can learn if the civilization had slaves, and they can learn how many gods they believed in.

Ancient Egypt had lots of different kinds of art, but most of it was intended to show that the pharaoh was seen as a god. The ancient Egyptians believed that the pharaoh was divine, and they used their art to communicate that idea. The earliest art was pictures called **reliefs**. Reliefs were carved into stone, but instead of carving the picture, the artist carved away everything except the picture. It makes the image stand out from the stone.

They also painted the inside of their tombs. The paintings show the deceased person enjoying the afterlife. The paintings also show some of the ordinary parts of ancient Egyptian life, like hunting and farming. This art has been preserved because it was shut up inside tombs for thousands of years. We can still see a lot of the original colors. As the people advanced their skills, the paintings became more and more detailed.

The ancient Egyptians also made **sculptures**. They usually made sculptures out of hard stone, and you can see many of their sculptures today. Ancient Egyptian sculptures face forward stiffly, and they show the real faces of people.

Ancient Egypt had lots of beautiful art, but it wasn't the only civilization creating art. Aksum also made a lot of art. We know it was different from ancient Egyptian art, but not as much of it survived. Aksum made pottery. It was usually decorated with **geometric patterns**. A geometric pattern is a shape that repeats itself many times. The most popular shape was the Christian cross, but other shapes were added to the pottery with stamps, decorative etching, and painting.

We don't have any statues from Aksum, but the bases that remain show its statues must have been impressive. Historians believe that one of the bases was intended to support a metal statue that was three times taller than a person. There are some smaller figurines of women and animals. Sadly, most of their art is now gone. Most of Aksum's tombs were looted. The little we have shows that Aksum made some impressive art during their time in ancient Africa.

Chapter 9 Activity Challenge

Can you identify which of these monuments are from ancient Africa?

The pyramids of Giza

The Colosseum

Stelae

Nubian pyramids

The Parthenon

Step Pyramid of Djoser at Saqqara

Stonehenge

The Great Sphinx

Chapter 10: Myths and Religion

Religion was a very important part of ancient Africa. The people had special religious practices. They also had myths about their gods, which helped them understand the world around them. In some ancient African civilizations, priests had a lot of power. They even had some power over the king! Each culture had its own religious practices, but there are some similarities between the different civilizations.

Ancient Egypt worshiped many different gods and goddesses. Some think that ancient Egypt had about two thousand different gods and goddesses. Can you imagine trying to remember all of those different deities? Each village had a specific god that they worshiped. **Horus** and **Osiris** were the most popular gods. Horus was the god of the sky. Osiris was the god of the afterlife.

The afterlife was very important to the ancient Egyptians. They believed that part of the soul called the **ka** remained in the body after death. The **ba** was the part that left the body at death. You need to have both the ka and the ba to still be you, so the Egyptians learned how to **mummify** bodies. They wanted to preserve the body to make sure that the person would have a good afterlife. Mummies were usually buried with jewels and food, which the Egyptians believed the soul would enjoy in the afterlife.

To get into the afterlife, you had to first go to the Hall of Truth. There, **Anubis** weighed your soul against an ostrich feather. Anubis was the god of the dead, but he was different from Osiris. If your soul was lighter than an ostrich feather, you got to go to the afterlife. If it was heavier, then it was eaten by **Ammit**, a demon with the head of a crocodile and the body of a lion. No one wanted to have their souls eaten, so the people tried to live good lives.

A picture of Ammit.
https://commons.wikimedia.org/wiki/File:Ammit_BD.jpg

The ancient Egyptians also believed the pharaoh was divine. When the pharaoh died, he or she would become a god. During their life, the pharaoh was the **mediator** (a person who communicates ideas between different groups of people) between the people and the gods. The priests helped with the temples and appeased the gods, but it was the pharaoh's responsibility to keep the gods happy.

Kush followed many of the same religious practices that ancient Egypt followed, especially early in its history. The people worshiped the same gods, and they took care to preserve people for the afterlife. They even built little pyramids as tombs. Between 350 BCE and 350 CE, some of the Kushites began to follow local gods. The most popular one was **Apedemak** (ah-pa-de-mak). He was the god of victory and good harvests.

Another traditional religion in Africa comes from the **Dogon** people (doh-gon). They still practice their traditional religion today in the country of **Mali** in West Africa. Their religion is mostly focused on the star Sirius, which they call **Po Tolo**.

The Dogon people have an important religious ceremony every sixty years. This event celebrates something that happened three thousand years ago. The Dogon people believe they were visited by beings from a planet near Sirius. The **Hogon** (ho-gun) is the main religious leader of each village. He dresses and acts to remind the people of the creation myth, which is very important to the Dogon culture.

Many ancient religions were built on mythology. Here are a few myths from the civilizations we have looked at in this book.

Kanaga mask.
Tropenmuseum, part of the National Museum of World Cultures, CC BY-SA 3.0
https://creativecommons.org/licenses/by-sa/3.0 via Wikimedia Commons
https://commons.wikimedia.org/wiki/File:COLLECTIE_TROPENMUSEUM_Houten_masker_TMnr_6372-2.jpg

Ancient Egyptian Creation

In the beginning, the universe was filled with darkness and chaos. There were no trees or people or even gods. Then, one day, a hill called the **Benben** appeared. The god **Atum** stood on the hill. He looked at the dark chaos and realized he was alone. That made Atum sad, so he created **Shu** and **Tefnut** (tef-nuht) by spitting. Shu and Tefnut then created the world by giving birth to two more **deities** (gods or goddesses). Their names were **Nut** and **Geb**. Nut was in charge of the sky, and Geb was in charge of the earth.

Nut and Geb were deeply in love, but the other gods didn't like it. Some versions of this myth say that Shu separated them, and some versions say Atum separated them. Either way, Nut was placed high in the sky. This separated Nut and Geb.

Nut eventually gave birth to five children. They were **Osiris**, **Isis**, **Set**, **Nephthys** (nef-this), and **Horus**. These were the five most popular gods in ancient Egypt. In the beginning, Osiris was made the king of Egypt. Humans were created by Atum's tears, and they lived on the earth that was formed by Nut and Geb.

A typical depiction of Amun, another important Egyptian god. He was the god of the sun and the air.

Jeff Dahl, CC BY-SA 4.0 https://creativecommons.org/licenses/by-sa/4.0 via Wikimedia Commons https://commons.wikimedia.org/wiki/File:Amun.svg

How Osiris Became the Ancient Egyptian God of the Afterlife

Osiris was known as the god of the afterlife, but he didn't start out that way. At first, Osiris was the king of Egypt. He was a good king.

Under his rule, Egypt was beautiful and peaceful. His brother **Set** was jealous. He wanted to be king and have all the power that Osiris had. So, he made a plan. He made a chest that fit Osiris. Then, he lured Osiris into the chest, slammed the lid shut, and threw it in the Nile River.

Isis was very upset about it. Osiris was her brother and her husband, and she didn't want him to die. When Isis found Osiris's body, she began working on bringing him back to life.

Set found out, and he was very angry. He went to the place Isis had hidden Osiris's body. He cut it up into forty-two pieces and hid the pieces all around Egypt. Isis had to go find all the pieces. By the time she was done, she was still missing a piece. It had been eaten by a fish! Even though she was able to bring Osiris back, he couldn't be the king of Egypt anymore. Instead, he became the king of the afterlife.

Outside of Egypt

There are many different deities, spirits, tricksters, and heroes in African mythology. For example, some tribes in East Africa called their main god **Mulungu** (ma-lun-gu). Some tribes of West Africa called their main god **Amma** or **Olorun** (o-lor-un).

For a long time, African mythology was not written down. While many civilizations and tribes had written languages, they either did not write down their myths, or those documents were lost to history. Instead, many people in Africa had an **oral tradition**. That means they told their stories verbally instead of writing them down. There were even professional storytellers. It was their job to remember all the stories and tell them to the people.

Historians are working on writing down the myths that people in Africa still tell. The mythology of Africa is as varied as its civilizations. As you now know, those civilizations were very important to the development of the ancient world.

Chapter 10 Activity Challenge

Can you choose the correct answer for each question?

| Dogon | Osiris | Mulungu | mummification |
| Amma | Apedemak | Atum | oral tradition |

1. The god of the ancient Egyptian afterlife was called _____.

2. The Hogon was a religious leader for the _____ people.

3. Ancient Egyptians used _____ to preserve the body for the afterlife.

4. The main god was called _____ by some West African tribes.

5. Some East African tribes called their main god _____.

6. The first god in ancient Egyptian mythology was _____.

7. A popular Kushite god was _____.

8. Much of Africa practiced an _____ when it came to telling their myths.

Part 3:

MEDIEVAL AFRICA FOR KIDS

A CAPTIVATING GUIDE TO MANSA MUSA, THE MALI EMPIRE, AND OTHER AFRICAN CIVILIZATIONS OF THE MIDDLE AGES

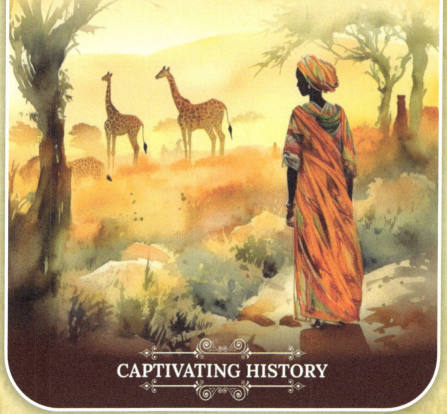

CAPTIVATING HISTORY

INTRODUCTION

You've probably heard about the Middle Ages. It was the time after the Roman Empire when Europe struggled to rebuild. There were knights and kings, and the Vikings attacked many towns across Europe.

When most of us think about the medieval era, we think about Europe. But have you ever wondered what the Middle Ages were like in other places? Medieval Africa was very different from Europe—in fact, it was much more powerful! Many empires ruled in Africa during this time, and they became wealthy due to trade. Africa had many natural resources, like salt and gold. Merchants traveled across the ocean and the Sahara Desert to trade with the African people. Many of these merchants were Muslims. During medieval Africa's history, Islam became an important part of daily life, but the African people did not just blindly accept a new religion. Instead, they took Islam, combined it with their traditional religions, and made something unique. Medieval Africa was full of creativity, innovation, scholarship, and riches that made the whole world take notice.

But how did medieval Africa make these trade connections? What did they do with all their wealth? How many empires were there, and how long were they powerful? Medieval Africa is full of questions like these.

Children and parents will enjoy reading this fun, up-to-date history of this long-forgotten area of medieval history. This book has everything you need to learn about the empires, rulers, and innovations that made medieval Africa powerful. Get ready to set off across history to discover cities of gold and the people who called Africa home.

Chapter 1: The African Middle Ages

When we think about the **Middle Ages**, most people think about Europe. The Middle Ages in Europe were hard and full of chaos. The people were trying to rebuild their lives after the fall of the Roman Empire, and that took a lot of time.

However, other places also had a medieval period, and they thrived! Instead of confusion and chaos, it was a time of growth and new discoveries. One of those places was **Africa**.

Historians study African history differently than history from other continents. We don't have many written documents from ancient or medieval Africa, even though there were many powerful kingdoms that impacted the world. Most of the written texts we have come from empires outside of Africa.

Fun Fact: A few African kingdoms, like Ethiopia, wrote a lot during the Middle Ages.

Of course, that doesn't mean that medieval Africa wasn't full of new discoveries and incredible art. In fact, much of the information we have about these kingdoms comes from **archeology**. The kingdoms left behind buildings and other objects that tell us a lot about their cultures, and historians use them to piece together medieval African history.

COOL FACT: Historians also use rock art and oral traditions to understand the Middle Ages in Africa. Oral traditions are stories that have been told many times over many generations.

This history was full of rich kingdoms and vibrant cultures. There were many different kingdoms.

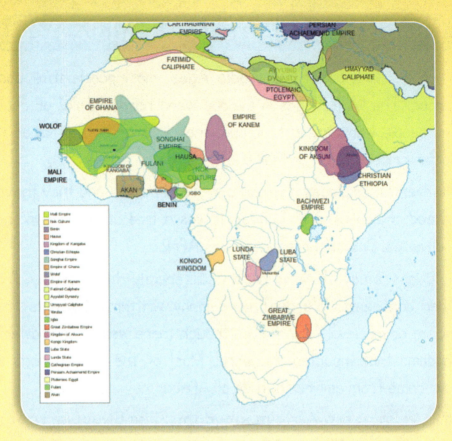

Map of Ancient & Medieval Sub-Saharan African States
Jeff Israel (ZyMOS), CC BY-SA 3.0 <https://creativecommons.org/licenses/by-sa/3.0>,
via Wikimedia Commons https://commons.wikimedia.org/wiki/File:African-civilizations-map-pre-colonial.svg

Most historians say the Middle Ages lasted from about 500 CE to 1500 CE. That's about a thousand years! Africa was very diverse, and a lot happened on the continent. Many of the kingdoms were powerful and rich.

One of the events that impacted the African Middle Ages was the spread of **Islam**. Islam is a world religion that believes in **God**. It started in the Middle East, but it has now spread all over the world. Muslims believe that God spoke to the prophet **Muhammad** and gave him new laws.

Fun Fact: Muhammad lived from 571 to 632 CE. By the time he died, many people were following Islam as their religion.

These new rules focus on **justice** and living in the right way. By the mid-600s, Islam had already spread to parts of northern Africa—and would continue to expand from there. You might think Islam spread across Africa in an orderly manner that is easy to follow. However, it is a little more complicated. Islam spread into Africa in several different areas, but it took a very long time to reach the whole continent. Towns and empires on the coast were first to adopt the religion. Sometimes, they even adapted it by adding their own traditions.

COOL FACT: People in central Africa did not learn about Islam until much later. Some of them did not encounter Islam until the 1800s!

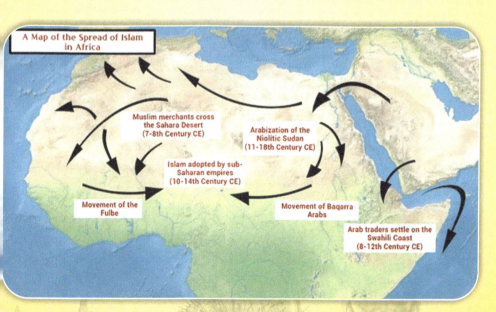

A map indicating the spread of Islam in Africa, 7th to 18th century CE

One of the main reasons Islam spread into Africa was for **trade**. Africa had a rich trade network both within and outside the continent. When the Muslim people came to Africa, they brought their religion with them.

Some kingdoms fully converted to Islam, like the **Mali Empire**. They used Islamic rules to make their laws and built many **mosques**.

COOL FACT: A mosque is an Islamic place of worship.

The Great Mosque of Kairouan, 670 CE.
https://commons.wikimedia.org/wiki/File:Great_Mosque_of_Kairouan.jpg#/media/File:Great_Mosque_of_Kairouan.jpg

Other empires, like the **Ghana Empire**, allowed people to convert to Islam, but the rulers never converted. These people allowed Islam and their traditional religions to exist together, so they both influenced each other. African empires converted or **tolerated** Islam because they wanted to continue trading. African leaders believed that adopting this outside religion would strengthen their ties to the merchants. It also helped increase their political power and improved **literacy**.

Fun Fact: The Muslim religious leaders taught people how to read. How do you think people learning how to read could help an empire?

In East Africa, the Islamic people also had to deal with **Christianity**. Christianity had become part of some African countries earlier, like **Nubia**. The Islamic people had to work very hard to convert the people in East Africa to Islam. It was not until the 1300s that many of the African people converted. Can you imagine working to convert someone to an idea or religion for centuries?

The roof of the 13th century rock-cut Church of Bete Giyorgis in Lalibela.
A. Davey from Where I Live Now: Pacific Northwest, CC BY 2.0 <https://creativecommons.org/licenses/by/2.0>, via Wikimedia Commons https://commons.wikimedia.org/wiki/File:The_Roof_Crosses,_Bet_Giyorgis,_Lalbela,_Ethiopia_(3278990293).jpg#/media/File:The_Roof_Crosses,_Bet_Giyorgis,_Lalbela,_Ethiopia_(3278990293).jpg

The African people got a lot more out of Islam than just a religious system. They also learned a new way to interact with the world.

Fun Fact: Islam is a religion, but it is also a legal and political system. When a country converts to Islam, it can implement laws that closely follow Muslim beliefs.

The people also received better access to trade. Africa was an important part of the trade routes during the Middle Ages, and much wealth came through the Middle East. Trade was a critical part of African culture during this period, and many of the kingdoms grew wealthy. They had important cities where merchants traveled to trade. Africa had a lot to offer the rest of the world!

COOL FACT: Africa traded things like salt and gold. Everyone wanted these things.

The Citadel of Gondershe, Somalia.
Warya, CC BY-SA 3.0 <https://creativecommons.org/licenses/by-sa/3.0>, via Wikimedia Commons; https://commons.wikimedia.org/wiki/File:Gondereshe2008.jpg

Even though Islam was important during the African Middle Ages, the people did not adopt it blindly. Instead, they adapted it to fit their traditions and culture. They blended the two cultures to make something unique. This usually included things like arts. African people already liked geometric designs, and this new religion encouraged it. The people created temples similarly to other Islamic areas, and they made art inspired by their new faith.

Interesting fact: Islam does not allow artists to draw animals or people. Instead, their art has shapes and patterns in it. Can you imagine making art without drawing people or animals?

Just because the African people adopted a new religion didn't mean they gave up their old beliefs. They still worshipped their ancestors and thought their leaders were at least semi-divine. The people made their beliefs their own!

One of the big changes Islam brought to Africa was the creation of a brand-new language. It was called **Kiswahili**. The Muslim people used it to teach people how to read the Koran.

COOL FACT: The Koran is one of the holy books of Islam. Reading the Koran is very important to Muslim people.

The people of Africa were adaptable. They accomplished so much, and their hard work has influenced our modern lives. Let's look at some of the most famous kingdoms in the African Middle Ages to see how the people on this continent thrived!

Chapter 1 Activity

Can you choose which achievements below came from the African Middle Ages?

- Built the Great Wall of China
- Developed a new language called Kiswahili
- Fought the Vikings
- Built big trading cities and traded gold and salt
- Had famous jousting tournaments
- Housed the Ghana and Mali Empires
- Adapted Islam to their traditions
- Were the first people to discover America

Chapter 2: The Ghana Empire

The Ghana Empire was a powerful kingdom built on trade. They were so important that people crossed the **Sahara Desert** to trade with them.

Fun Fact: The Sahara Desert is the largest warm desert in the world. It is about the size of the United States of America!

The Ghana Empire lasted from about 300 CE to 1200 CE. It was located in Western Africa near the **Niger River**. Today, three different countries control the land the Ghana Empire once ruled: Mali, Mauritania, and Senegal.

Interesting fact: There is a modern African country called Ghana, but it is not related to the Ghana Empire.

Map of the Ghana Empire
Luxo, CC BY-SA 3.0 <http://creativecommons.org/licenses/by-sa/3.0/>, via Wikimedia Commons https://commons.wikimedia.org/wiki/File:Ghana_empire_map.png

Historians think people have lived in West Africa since at least the **Neolithic Period**. Archeologists have found old buildings from the Iron Age, and there was a lot of copper in the area. The metal let the people make tools, and the farmlands let people grow crops. Eventually, the people developed into tribes, and one of them was called the **Soninke people**. They united together under **Dinga Cisse** and started the Ghana Empire.

Historians don't know much about how the Ghana Empire worked in its early days. There aren't a lot of written documents, and archeology can't tell us everything about a culture.

COOL FACT: The people of Ancient Ghana did not call their kingdom "Ghana." People outside the empire called it that. "Ghana" was a Soninke word that meant "warrior king." The people who lived in the Ghana Empire called it "Wagadou."

The Ghana Empire had a different political structure than modern Western countries. They did not have a big central government. Instead, they had many villages that were all ruled by a king. The king was an **absolute monarch**, which meant he had all the power and no one could question him. He was in charge of justice and religion. The people treated him with extra care and even made sacrifices in the king's honor. Can you imagine how much the king had to worry about? How would you run a religion if you were in charge?

Most people in Ghana were farmers, but they did not own their land. Instead, each family got a section from the village leader. People grew food like sweet potatoes and grains like rice and millet. The land was good for farming because the Niger River ran through the kingdom. The river also provided fish and birds, so the people usually had plenty to eat.

Interesting fact: The king and village leaders lived in the best houses, but most people lived in one-story houses made of mud bricks, wood, and stone. The houses were so effective that people still build houses like this in the area today!

The most important part of the Ghana Empire was the trade routes. They made all their wealth and power because they were on two trade routes. One of those routes ran north to south, and the other ran east to west. The second network of routes was called the **Trans-Saharan Trade Route**.

Fun Fact: The Trans-Saharan Trade Route was at least 600 miles long! People had to cross on foot or in camel caravans.

The people of Ancient Ghana traded with Muslim merchants in big cities. The more they traded, the more powerful they became. Soon, they expanded the empire by taking over smaller kingdoms and tribes around them.

Chinguetti, Ghana Empire.
François COLIN, CC BY-SA 2.5 <https://creativecommons.org/licenses/by-sa/2.5>, via Wikimedia Commons; https://commons.wikimedia.org/wiki/File:Chinguetti-Vue_Goblale_Vieille_ville.jpg

The capital of the Ghana Empire was **Koumbi Saleh**. Historians believe it was a huge city, especially for the medieval era. It took up about 110 acres, and many small villages were around it. A lot of trade took place in the capital. Because many of the traders were Muslim, there was a separate side of the city for them starting in the middle of the 11th century. The Muslim side has twelve mosques! The other side had shrines for the empire's traditional religion. Even though they had different religions, the Ghana Empire and the Islamic traders still worked together.

Koumbi Saleh, Mauritania.
Eric Gaba (Sting - fr:Sting), CC BY-SA 3.0 <https://creativecommons.org/licenses/by-sa/3.0>, via Wikimedia Commons; https://commons.wikimedia.org/wiki/File:Mauritania_location_map.svg

The Ghana Empire traded many different goods, but the most valuable thing they traded was **gold**. The gold mines were south of the early Ghana Empire. For years, the Ghana people traded with the kingdoms south of them to get gold, but as they became more powerful, they expanded their empire and took over the gold mines.

Interesting fact: The kings were very protective of their gold. The king was the only person who could have gold nuggets—the merchants had to use gold dust instead.

Although gold was the most precious item, the Ghana Empire traded other things. Another important item for trade was **salt**. We might not think salt is very important. It helps food taste good sometimes, but how else does salt affect our daily lives?

For the people in the medieval era, salt was very important. They did not have refrigeration back then, so they used salt to preserve food.

COOL FACT: People need to eat some salt daily to stay healthy. Luckily, most of us get enough salt every day from our food, so we don't have to worry about it like the people of the Middle Ages did.

The kingdoms north of Ghana had salt mines. They would mine the salt and then bring it to Ghana to trade. Salt was so important to the people that they sometimes used it as money, just like gold!

The empire also traded goods like ivory, ostrich feathers, and enslaved people. Slavery is not okay, but it was part of the Middle Ages. In return, the empire received copper, horses, and expensive fabrics. Trade networks quickly made Ghana rich!

Fun Fact: The Ghana Empire made a lot of money by taxing things that came in and out of their country. That meant everything was taxed twice!

Sadly, the Ghana Empire could not last forever. In the second half of the 11th century, the Islamic people in the north decided to **convert** their neighbors to Islam. When Ghana refused to change its religion to Islam, the Muslim forces attacked them several times. The Muslim forces were called the **Almoravids**. They briefly took over the empire but didn't have enough power to keep it. However, the Ghana Empire never recovered. They had lost a lot of the trade they needed to survive.

Ghana continued to decline into the 12th century. New trade routes opened elsewhere, so people didn't visit the Ghana Empire as much. There was also a bad drought for a few years, and the people struggled to grow food. There was a lot of tension, and civil wars broke out. Can you imagine living in the Ghana Empire during this time? It would have been very hard.

The Ghana Empire continued to crumble until it was absorbed by the Mali Empire. Even though the Ghana Empire is not here today, it was a very important part of medieval Africa. Its people were strong and wealthy because they were good traders.

Chapter 2 Activity

Can you identify which statements are true and which are false?

1. The Ghana Empire was founded by King Soninke.
2. The capital of the Kingdom of Ghana was Koumbi Saleh.
3. The Soninke people were the enemies of the Ghana Empire.
4. After its fall, the Ghana Empire became a part of the Kanem-Bornu Empire.
5. The Ghana Empire made its wealth by trading items like gold and salt.
6. Christians had their own part of the Ghana capital because they traded a lot with the empire.
7. Ghana fell because it was invaded by the Roman Empire.
8. The Ghana Empire was part of the Trans-Saharan Trade Route.

Chapter 3: The Kanem-Bornu Empire

The **Kanem-Bornu Empire** lasted over a thousand years. Its boundaries have changed many times, but it was in a good position on the **Trans-Saharan** Trade Route. The empire stayed in the center of Africa on the eastern shore of **Lake Chad**, even though it went through a lot of change.

COOL FACT: A part of the Kanem-Bornu Empire is still here today! It is called the Borno Emirate, but its people live under the governance of the other countries in the area.

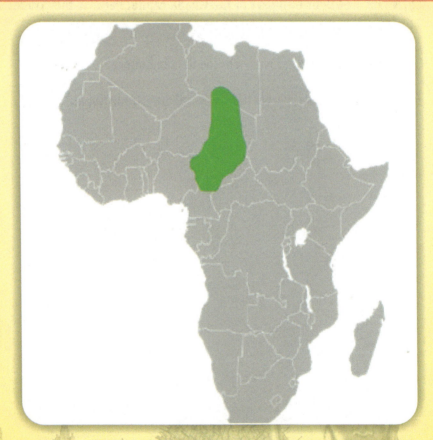

Map of the Kanem–Bornu Empire.
ArnoldPlaton, CC0, via Wikimedia Commons;
https://commons.wikimedia.org/wiki/File:Kanem-Bornu.svg#/media/File:Kanem-Bornu.svg

Before the Kanem-Bornu Empire began, **nomadic** people called the **Zaghawa** and the **Kanembu** were living in the area. Historians think these tribes used to wander in the **Sahara Desert**.

Interesting fact: Back then, the Sahara Desert wasn't as big or desert-like as it is today. Instead, it went through desiccation, which is when all the moisture comes out of something. As the water left the area, the people did, too.

The tribes migrated south and settled on the east side of **Lake Chad**. The Kanembu people started the Kanem Empire around 700 CE. However, it took them a long time to build cities. By the 10th century, it only had two towns, but it was still a very powerful kingdom.

One of the reasons the Kanem Empire became so important is that it was part of the **Trans-Saharan Trade Route**. This empire connected North Africa to Central Africa. It traded many things, like salt, copper, cotton, ostrich feathers, and gold. However, its biggest export was enslaved people, many of whom died trying to get across the Trans-Saharan Trade Route.

Interesting fact: Many of the people who were captured and forced into slavery came from south of the Kanem-Bornu Empire.

The first king of the Kanem Empire was **Sef, or Saif**, and his son was **Dugu**. Dugu started the **Duguwa** dynasty. Instead of calling their rulers kings, the Kanem people called them "**mais**."

Fun Fact: The Kanem people thought their kings were divine. They thought the mais could bring illnesses or health—and even life or death! Can you imagine having that much power?

The mais were powerful rulers, and many wanted to expand the Kanem Empire. They had a strong **cavalry**, partly because many people were still nomadic. The cavalry gave their military extra strength.

Expansion and connection to the trade routes brought **Islam** into the Kanem Empire. Around 1085 CE, the Saifawas **deposed** the last king of the Duguwa dynasty. The Saifawas were Muslim and started their own dynasty called the **Sefuwa dynasty**.

Fun Fact: The Sefuwa dynasty made Islam the court and state policy.

The people of the Kanem Empire didn't want to convert to Islam at first. They wanted to keep their old religion. Historians don't know exactly when the Kanem-Bornu Empire became Muslim, but it was popular among the people by the early 1200s.

Fun Fact: In medieval Africa, the people didn't always have the same religion as their king. It was normal for kings to convert to Islam, but the people still practiced their traditional religions. That's one reason the African people were able to adapt Islam to their way of life—there were many other religious influences at the same time!

The Kanem Empire continued to expand. One of its most famous leaders was **Mai Dunama Dabbalemi**, who ruled from 1210 to 1259 CE. He started diplomatic exchanges with the North African sultan; he also created a special hostel in Cairo to help fellow Muslims going to Mecca.

Fun Fact: Muslims believe they should take a trip to Mecca at least once in their lives. Mecca is an important holy city for them. These special religious trips are called pilgrimages.

Mai Dunama Dabbalemi is most famous for declaring **jihad** on the tribes around the Kanem Empire.

Interesting fact: A jihad is a religious war.

Dabbalemi fought for over seven years and conquered a lot of land. However, he also attacked the **Mune religion**, which made the Tubu and the **Bulala** people angry. The Tubu people didn't fight for long, but the Bulala people fought so much that they accidentally helped start the Bornu Empire.

Flag of Bornu Empire.
https://commons.wikimedia.org/wiki/File:Flag_of_the_Bornu_Empire.svg

Around 1400 CE, there was increasing unrest in Kanem due to civil wars. The Bulala people finally forced the Kanem leader to leave. His name was **Mai Uma b. Idris**. When Mai Idris fled to the west side of Lake Chad, the Kanem rulers became the rulers of **Bornu**, too.

Fun Fact: The people living in Bornu intermarried with the Kanem people. This created a new culture and group of people called the Kanuri.

It took many years for the Kanuri people to settle in Bornu, but once they did, they were stronger than ever. In the early 1500s, they were strong enough to push the Bulala out of Kanem and take back their land.

Group of Kanem-Bu warriors.
https://commons.wikimedia.org/wiki/File:Group_of_Kanem-Bu_warriors.jpg

The Kanem-Bornu Empire was strongest under **Mai Idris Alawma**. He ruled from around 1564 to 1596. Under his rule, the empire was the biggest it would ever be. He made changes to the army to make it better often used a **scorched earth policy** to help his conquests.

> **Interesting fact:** Scorched earth policy is when an attacking army burns all the plants in an area. They do this because they don't want the defending army to be able to get food in the wild. It makes people much more dependent on supply lines, which are easier to attack.

Mai Alawma was more than a good military leader who consolidated the empire. He also reformed the government and made the Kanem-Bornu kingdom rich and strong. He even built several new mosques! His hard work made the Kanem-Bornu kingdom strong until the mid-1600s.

The Kanem-Bornu Empire gradually began to fade. They slowly shrank, but it was an important place for Islamic learning in the 17th and 18th centuries. Sadly, even this couldn't save them. The **Fulani** people attacked them in the 1700s, and Kanem-Bornu Empire declined.

The Kanem-Bornu Empire ended around 1900, but it still exists today as Borno Emirate. The Kanuri people were strong and impacted much of African history, leaving a big mark on medieval Africa.

Chapter 3 Activity

Can you put these events in the right order?

1. The reign of King Idris Alawma.

2. The empire was founded by the Zaghawa and Kanembu nomadic people.

3. The Kanem Empire expanded under Mai Dunama Dabbalemi.

4. The Kanuri people recaptured the lost territories and became the Kanem-Bornu Empire.

5. Dugu started the Duguwa dynasty.

6. The Kanem-Bornu Empire ended and became the Borno Emirate.

Chapter 4: The Kingdom of Benin

The **Kingdom of Benin** was a powerful kingdom in West Africa. It was so powerful that European countries like Portugal and Great Britain wanted to trade with it! The Kingdom of Benin was located in the southern part of modern **Nigeria** and ruled from around 1200 CE to 1897 CE.

Fun Fact: The Kingdom of Benin is sometimes called the Kingdom of Edo.

Map of the Kingdom of Benin

The land had a lot of forests, including rainforests, dry forests, and even swamps! According to Benin history, this kingdom began with the **Edo people**. They were tired of their kings, the **Ogisos**, and asked **Prince Oranmiyan** to rule them instead.

Prince Oranmiyan was from the **Kingdom of Ife**. Ife was nearby, but it ruled slightly earlier than the Kingdom of Benin. Ife existed from about 1000 CE to the 1400s CE.

COOL FACT: The Kingdom of Ife was famous for its bronze work. Its people were best at making sculpted heads. Some historians think Ife's culture influenced Benin's as it developed.

Although Prince Oranmiyan was invited to rule the Edo people, the first king of Benin was **Eweka**. Eweka was Prince Oranmiyan's son.

Fun Fact: The Benin people called their king the oba.

Of course, the Kingdom of Benin was not big or powerful when Eweka ruled. He was the first oba! For many years, the political structure was a little complicated. Princes and tribal chiefs ruled some of the land—and some of these chiefs sent tribute to the king.

The **oba** of Benin was a little different from how we might think of a king today. The Benin oba had a divine right to rule.

Interesting fact: The people had many rituals to honor the oba, and one of them was human sacrifice. This was part of their culture until 1897!

The oba was also in charge of all trade with outside powers. Because of Benin's location, it was a good midpoint on trade routes. Benin **facilitated** trade between many African kingdoms, trading things like cotton, yams, salt, and cows.

Around 1450, the **Portuguese** began sailing down the coast of Africa, looking for gold. Although Benin didn't have gold, it did start trading with Portugal. Suddenly, the Kingdom of Benin grew and became very successful because of all this trade. The people traded pepper, ivory, and palm oil with the Europeans.

Sadly, much of Benin's success also came from the **slave trade**. During this time in its history, the Benin kingdom was expanding. The people conquered their neighbors and took the land for their own kingdom. Some tribes willingly sent tribute, including people for slavery, but other tribes were conquered. When Benin attacked a rival tribe, it captured people to sell to Western traders as enslaved people.

Interesting fact: The Western World refers to Europe and America. By the 1600s and 1700s, enslaved people were being moved to the Americas and Europe.

The Kingdom of Benin continued to expand. One of its greatest kings was **Oba Ewuare the Great.** He ruled from 1440 to 1473 CE and was famous as a warrior and magician. Under Ewuare, the role of the oba became **hereditary**.

COOL FACT: A hereditary position is a job or role passed on from parent to child. Usually, sons inherited from their fathers.

Depiction of Benin City.
https://commons.wikimedia.org/wiki/File:Ancient_Benin_city.JPG

Oba Ewuare also expanded the Kingdom of Benin to its largest size. Under his rule, the kingdom became very powerful, and he also rebuilt the capital, **Benin City**.

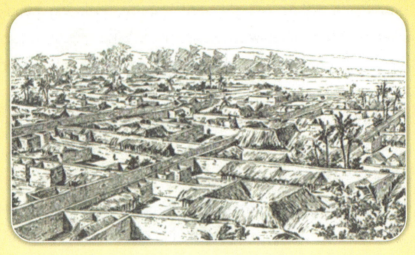

Drawing of Benin City.
https://commons.wikimedia.org/wiki/File:
Drawing_of_Benin_City_made_by_an_English_officer_1897.jpg

However, the most impressive part of Benin City comes from the royal palace. Many of the pillars in the palace were covered with **brass plaques**. These plaques weren't just pieces of metal, though. They were unique carvings and works of art that told the story of the Benin people.

Single-figure plaque, Benin Kingdom.
https://commons.wikimedia.org/wiki/File:Single-figure_plaque,_Benin_Kingdom_court_style,_Edo_peoples,_Benin_City,_Nigeria,_mid_16th_to_17th_century,_cast_copper_alloy_-_Dallas_Museum_of_Art_-_DSC04934.jpg

COOL FACT: These pieces of art are also called bronze plaques because brass and bronze are so similar.

Many of the brass plaques we still have were most likely made between 1550 and 1650. The artistic pieces have lots of detail, which amazed the Europeans when they first saw them. The Benin people made their art without European influences, proving the people of medieval Africa were full of creativity and innovation.

The plaques show the greatness of the oba. Although they don't tell us anything about commoners or women and children, they show us a lot about how the oba's palace functioned. Because of them, we have a record of many of the obas' achievements through the years. They also show warriors and important battles.

Interesting fact: Many of Benin's brass plaques are now in museums worldwide. You can see them at the British Museum, in Chicago, and even in Berlin!

Benin Kingdom - Warrior and Attendants.
Julia Manzerova, CC BY-SA 2.0 <https://creativecommons.org/licenses/by-sa/2.0>,
ia Wikimedia Commons; https://commons.wikimedia.org/wiki/File:Benin_kingdom_-_Warrior_and_attendants.jpg

The Kingdom of Benin had beautiful art and left an important impact on West Africa. Sadly, the Kingdom of Benin is not in Africa anymore. In the 1700s and 1800s, Benin began to struggle. The royal family started civil wars for the throne, which weakened the government and economy. Can you imagine trying to keep a strong trade network with wars happening around you? It would be chaos!

There were several weak rulers during this time. They tried to keep Western influences away with their religious rituals, but it wasn't enough to stop the British. The British wanted to control trade in West Africa. When the Kingdom of Benin didn't welcome their merchants, the British invaded. They took Benin City in 1897, burning it. The Kingdom of Benin was officially over.

COOL FACT: Even though the Kingdom of Benin ended in 1897, it eventually became the Republic of Benin in modern Nigeria. Benin City still exists today, and the oba of the city advises the Nigerian government. The oba is no longer king, but he's still important.

The Kingdom of Benin ruled for almost 700 years. In that time, it shaped medieval Africa by creating a strong trade relationship with other kingdoms and the Western World. It also created beautiful art that continues to amaze people today.

Chapter 4 Activity

Can you solve the multiple-choice questions below? Be sure to look over the chapter for the answers!

1. What is another common name for the Kingdom of Benin?

   A) Kingdom of Ethiopia   B) Kingdom of Axum   C) Kingdom of Edo

2. Who first established the Kingdom of Benin?

   A) Oba Ewuare the Great   B) the Edo people   C) King Solomon

3. What was the capital of the kingdom?

   A) Benin City   B) Ife   C) Timbuktu

4. Who conquered the Kingdom of Benin?

   A) The French   B) The Egyptians   C) The British

5. What kind of art is Benin most famous for?

   A) Paintings   B) Brass plaques   C) Stone sculptures

Chapter 5: The Mali Empire

The **Mali Empire** was huge and wealthy. It ruled much of West Africa from around 1235 CE to 1670 CE. At the height of its power, it had one of the largest armies in the world at that time and was a critical part of the trade networks.

Fun Fact: The Mali Empire is also called the Manding Empire after the people who started it. They were the Mandingo people (also called the Malinke people).

The Mali Empire stretched across many modern countries like Mali, Niger, Guinea, and The Gambia.

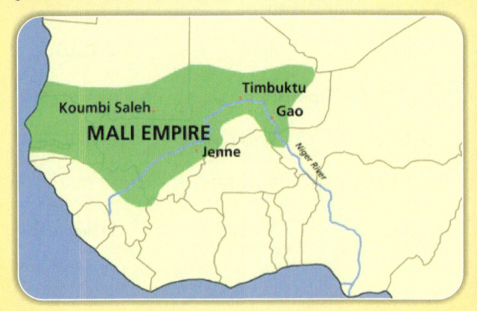

Map of the Mali Empire.
This file is licensed under the Creative Commons Attribution-Share Alike 3.0 Unported license; https://commons.wikimedia.org/wiki/File:MALI_empire_map.PNG

The Malinke people had lived in the area for many years, and they helped the **Ghana Empire** with the gold trade near the end of that empire's reign. As Ghana crumbled at the end of the 1100s, the **Kingdom of Sosso** took over most of the land.

Fun Fact: The Kingdom of Sosso is also called the Kingdom of Susu.

Their ruler was **King Sumanguru**, who started his reign around 1200 CE. He was a bad ruler and was harsh, even imposing trade limits on the Malinke people! The Malinke people were upset about this, so one of their princes named **Sundiata Keita** rose up against the Kingdom of Sosso. He made alliances with other local leaders and defeated the Kingdom of Sosso in 1235 at the Battle of **Krina (or Kirina)**. The Mali Empire had begun, and the land Sundiata Keita won made Mali the largest empire at the time. Throughout the first part of its history, Mali continued to grow to cover about 1,200 miles.

Interesting fact: Sundiata named his empire "Mali." It means "the place where the king lives."

Sundiata also helped set up the Mali Empire's government. The king was an absolute monarch. He had advisors and nobility under his rule, but the king was in charge of running the government and controlling trade.

Fun Fact: The king of the Mali Empire was called the Mansa. The Mansa was always chosen from the Keita clan, but the king's oldest son was not always the next ruler. Can you imagine how much chaos that caused when it was time for a new king?

Trade was very important to the Mali Empire. They were in a perfect place for trade—the Mali Empire even took over areas rich in gold to make its trade even more valuable. Some of these areas were **Galam**, **Bambuk**, and **Bure**.

However, having gold was only one way the Mali Empire made its vast fortune. It also taxed goods as they came through the empire and sold goods it purchased for higher prices. The Mali Empire also took over **Timbuktu**, an important trade port.

> COOL FACT: Timbuktu was started by nomadic people called the Tuaregs around 1100 CE. It was on the Niger River and was a good starting point for the Trans-Saharan Trade Route.

Because of all this trade, the Mali Empire attracted Islamic traders. Of course, Islam had already been in the area, but it eventually became an important part of the empire. The Mansas converted to Islam, but they did not force the commoners to convert. Instead, many people converted on their own. They combined Islam with their traditional **animist** religions to create something unique. As the empire became more powerful, more Islamic scholars and **missionaries** moved to Mali.

The Great Mosque of Djenné, Mali.
Andy Gilham, CC BY-SA 3.0 <http://creativecommons.org/licenses/by-sa/3.0/>, via Wikimedia Commons; https://commons.wikimedia.org/wiki/File:Great_Mosque_of_Djenn%C3%A9_1.jpg

Islam became very popular under **Mansa Musa I**. Musa I was one of the most famous kings in medieval Africa. He used his huge army to double the Mali Empire's land.

Djenné Terracotta archer.
https://commons.wikimedia.org/wiki/File:Djenne_Terracotta_Archer_(13th-15th_cent).jpg#/media/File:Djenne_Terracotta_Archer_(13th-15th_cent).jpg

Fun Fact: Historians think Mansa Musa I's army had about 100,000 soldiers and 10,000 horses. Can you imagine having a group that big?

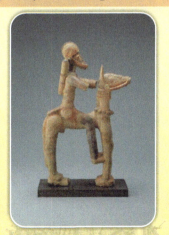

Djenné Terracotta equestrian.
https://commons.wikimedia.org/wiki/File:Djenne_Terracotta_Equestrian_(13th-15th_cent).jpg

We'll look into the details of Mansa Musa's life in the next chapter, but when Musa I died around 1332 CE, the Mali Empire was in its **golden age.** He did a lot for Mali. He made the government stronger and brought in a lot of wealth.

COOL FACT: Mansa Musa I was one of the richest people in the history of the world. What would you do if you were one of the richest people today?

He also made a famous **pilgrimage** to **Mecca** in 1324. He gave away so much gold that people were amazed and wanted to visit Mali. When he came back, Musa brought architects, teachers, and poets with him. He wanted Mali to be an important cultural center as well as rich and politically powerful. Musa shaped cities like **Gao** and Timbuktu into major cultural centers. Timbuktu even had a famous school called the **University of Sankore**.

The Djinguereber Mosque, 1327.
KaTeznik, CC BY-SA 2.0 FR <https://creativecommons.org/licenses/by-sa/2.0/fr/deed.en>, via Wikimedia Commons; https://commons.wikimedia.org/wiki/File:Djingareiber_cour.jpg

Mansa Musa even built mosques! One of those mosques was **Djinguereber**, also known as the Great Mosque of Timbuktu.

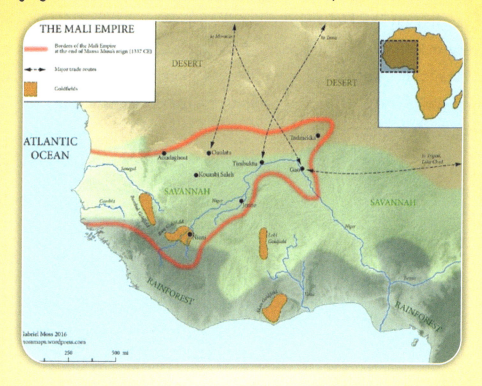

The Mali Empire at the time of Mansa Musa's death.
Gabriel Moss, CC BY-SA 4.0 <https://creativecommons.org/licenses/by-sa/4.0>, via Wikimedia Commons; https://commons.wikimedia.org/wiki/File:The_Mali_Empire.jpg#/media/File:The_Mali_Empire.jpg

However, the Mali Empire was not able to hold onto its golden age for long. Soon after Musa died, the Mali Empire began losing control of its borderlands. Other groups, like the **Tuareg** and the **Mossi**, attacked, gradually taking over areas. The empire also slipped into civil wars over succession. Because it wasn't clear which relative should be king next, people fought each other for the throne. How do you think that could weaken an empire?

The Mali Empire faded. New trade routes opened up, and these threatened Mali's economy. By 1550, Mali was no longer powerful.

In 1610, Mahmud IV died as the last king. The Mali Empire was over—it was taken into the **Moroccan Empire**.

Even though the Mali Empire is no longer around today, it was still very important. The Mali people built schools and built up impressive amounts of wealth. The empire also made a lasting mark on medieval Africa. It was important to global development, so its legacy still impacts us today.

Chapter 5 Activity

Can you match the king to his achievements? A king might have multiple achievements listed.

| Mahmud IV | Sundiata Keita | Mansa Musa I |

- United the tribes of the Malinke peoples and formed the Mali Empire

- Developed cities like Timbuktu and Gao into important cultural centers and improved the Mali Empire

- Was the last king of the Mali Empire

- Named the Mali Empire

- Built Djinguereber, the Great Mosque of Timbuktu

Chapter 6: Emperor Mansa Musa

Mansa Musa I was one of the most famous African rulers from the medieval era. He came to the throne of the **Mali Empire** around 1312 CE. He led the Mali Empire through its golden age and was famous for his great wealth. Under his rule, the Mali Empire became a great place of learning and creativity.

Fun Fact: Musa is the Arabic form of the name Moses. Moses was an important Israelite leader, and Jews, Christians, and Muslims still honor him today.

Ruler Mansa Musa.
HistoryNmoor, CC BY-SA 4.0 <https://creativecommons.org/licenses/by-sa/4.0/>, via Wikimedia Commons; https://commons.wikimedia.org/wiki/File:Empire_mansa_musa.jpeg

The king before Mansa Musa was **Muhammad ibn Qu**. Some stories say Muhammad wanted to explore the Atlantic Ocean and set out on a voyage. Muhammad made Musa the ruler until he returned, but then he never came back. Thus, Musa became the next Mansa.

Interesting fact: Not all historians agree with this story. Some think Mansa made up this story after getting rid of Muhammad, but no one knows for sure.

Mansa Musa I was young when he became the leader of the Mali Empire. Historians think he was in his early twenties. Can you imagine running a huge empire as a young adult?

He spent most of his early reign expanding the empire. His army was huge! It had about 100,000 soldiers and 10,000 horses. With his huge army, Musa doubled the Mali Empire.

COOL FACT: **The Mali Empire was the second-largest empire in the world at the time. It was only smaller than the Mongol Empire.**

He knew he needed help governing all of this land, so he set up provinces ruled by governors. His administration did more recordkeeping that was all sent to **Niani**, the capital, and worked hard to improve the cities. Musa made the empire even more wealthy by increasing taxes, making conquered tribes pay tribute, and using Mali's gold and copper mines.

While Mansa Musa I was conquering the tribes and cities around him, he also captured people. Many of these people became enslaved. Slavery was another way the Mali Empire gained wealth, but it was still wrong.

Seventeen years into his reign, Musa I decided to take a **pilgrimage** to **Mecca**. He left the Mali Empire in 1324 with an impressive **entourage**. An entourage is a group of people who help a specific person, usually someone famous or important. Musa's entourage had about 60,000 people!

Fun Fact: Musa brought a lot of gold with him. He also paid for everything the people and animals on the trip needed. Can you imagine how much that cost?

Travel during the Middle Ages was different than travel today. People could not drive down highways or take flights. Instead, people had to walk or ride animals everywhere. Musa rode a horse and brought at least eighty camels with him on his trip to Mecca.

Fun Fact: His trip to Mecca and back was at least 4,000 miles. How long do you think it would take to walk that far?

Mansa Musa on his way to Mecca, c. 1670.
https://commons.wikimedia.org/wiki/File:Mansa-Musa-on-his-way-to-Mecca-Credit-Print-Collector-Getty-images-1536x790.jpg

Musa made a huge impact when he arrived in **Cairo**, Egypt, in July 1324. He was generous and polite, but his journey was about more than just going to Mecca. He was also showing off his empire's wealth, which intrigued people across the Middle East and Europe. It made people want to visit the Mali Empire.

Mansa Musa I stayed in Cairo for three months. He met with the Cairo leader named **al-Nasir Muhammad**. Their first meeting was tense. Al-Nasir wanted Musa to pay **homage**.

> **COOL FACT:** Homage is a special way of giving honor or respect to somebody. Al-Nasir wanted Musa to bow down before him. Musa finally agreed if he was really bowing to Allah, the Arabian name for God.

Thankfully, the two rulers became more friendly after that. Musa had a palace while he stayed in Cairo, and his entourage spent lots of gold in the marketplaces. They spent and gave away so much gold that they actually decreased its value for about twelve years.

In October 1324, Musa continued his journey to Mecca, where he bought land to help future people from Mali make pilgrimages. He was impressed with the holy buildings in Mecca and decided he wanted similar buildings in Mali.

> **COOL FACT:** While Musa was making his pilgrimage, his general, Sagmandia, conquered the city of Gao for Mali. When Musa returned, both Gao and Timbuktu submitted to his authority.

Musa brought back architects and scholars to make the Mali Empire even better. He ordered several mosques to be built in Gao and Timbuktu. The most famous mosque was the **Great Mosque** in Timbuktu. It is also called the **Djinguereber**. The building was completed around 1330 and made from beaten earth supported by wood. The wood usually sticks out of the building, which makes Mali's architecture unique.

Musa did more than just construct beautiful buildings, though. He also wanted people to be avid learners, so he created schools and universities. In Timbuktu, the **University of Sankore** became a center of learning for things like religion, math, and astronomy. The city soon became famous for trade, learning, and Islamic activities, and people hurried to visit.

Education and more religious devotion were big parts of Mansa Musa's reign. He led the Mali Empire through the best time in its history, making it large and powerful. However, one of Mansa Musa I's biggest impacts on world history was his pilgrimage. He showed off Mali's wealth so effectively that people soon spread the word about it. The stories even reached Europe. In 1375, a Spanish mapmaker created the *Catalan Atlas*. It is a map of West Africa, and it shows Musa sitting on his throne with gold all around him.

Musa depicted holding an imperial golden globe, 1375.
https://commons.wikimedia.org/wiki/File:Catalan_Atlas_BNF_Sheet_6_Mansa_Musa_(cropped).jpg

The Europeans were fascinated by the legendary amounts of gold in Mali. Their curiosity eventually led to explorations. They sailed across the seas, looking for new trade routes and lands. Mansa Musa's pilgrimage ended up changing the world forever.

Interesting fact: Historians don't know exactly when Musa died. Some historians think he died in 1332 CE, but some think he died in 1337 CE.

The Mali Empire lasted long after Mansa Musa died, but it would never be the same. His work changed the empire and the world, inspiring people to search for wealth and to hold to their religious ideas.

Chapter 6 Activity

Can you put these events in timeline order?

1. The pilgrimage to Mecca.

2. Mansa Musa started his reign.

3. The Catalan Atlas was made with Musa on it.

4. He revitalized and improved cities.

5. He built the Great Mosque at Timbuktu.

6. Sagmandia conquered Gao.

Chapter 7: The Kingdom of Abyssinia

The **Kingdom of Abyssinia** ruled from about 1270 CE to 1974 in modern-day **Ethiopia**. This country is in East Africa, and it has a very long history. In fact, Ethiopia is one of the oldest countries in the world!

Fun Fact: The Kingdom of Abyssinia is also called the Kingdom of Ethiopia.

Map of Abyssinia
https://commons.wikimedia.org/wiki/File:1818_Pinkerton_Map_of_Nubia,_Sudan_and_Abyssinia_-_Geographicus_-_Abyssinia-pinkerton-1818.jpg

Two kingdoms ruled the area before the Kingdom of Abyssinia. The first was the **Kingdom of Axum**. They ruled from the 1st century CE until the 8th century CE. Axum was the first sub-Saharan country to adopt Christianity, and they were so dedicated to it that people have practiced Christianity there ever since.

Fun Fact: The Kingdom of Abyssinia was one of the few predominately Christian kingdoms in medieval Africa.

After Axum faded, the **Zagwe dynasty** took over the area. It ruled the area until 1270 CE and expanded Ethiopian lands. Zagwe was also a Christian kingdom, and churches were important to the people.

COOL FACT: Ethiopia was safe from Muslim armies for a long time because it had been hospitable during Muhammad's lifetime. The Ethiopian people were allowed to practice Christianity without pressure to convert to Islam like many countries around them.

The most famous king of Zagwe was **Gebre Mesqel Lalibela**. He carved churches out of rock, which impressed the people. One of the most famous is the Church of Saint George at Lalibela. It was carved in the shape of a cross.

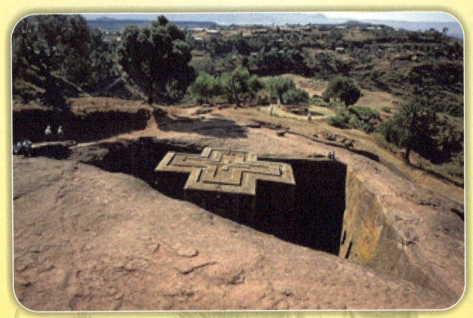

Church of Saint George at Lalibela, Ethiopia, 11-12th century CE.
Jialiang Gao www.peace-on-earth.org, CC BY-SA 3.0 <http://creativecommons.org/licenses/by-sa/3.0/>, via Wikimedia Commons; https://commons.wikimedia.org/wiki/File:Bete_Giyorgis_Lalibela_Ethiopia.jpg?uselang=de#fi

In 1270, the **Solomonid dynasty** ended the Zagwe dynasty and started the Kingdom of Abyssinia. The Solomonid dynasty claimed they were descended from King Solomon and the Queen of Sheba.

Interesting fact: King Solomon was an Israelite king recorded in the Old Testament of the Bible. The Queen of Sheba came to visit him. The Solomonid dynasty believes the two had a child named Menelik, who started the dynasty.

In 1270 CE, the dynasty was led by **Yekuno Amlak**. He overthrew the last Zagwe king and started his own kingdom.

Contemporary portrait of Yekuno Amlak, founder of the Ethiopian Empire.
https://commons.wikimedia.org/wiki/File:Yekuno_Amlak.png#/media/File:Yekuno_Amlak.png

Like many other countries, the Kingdom of Abyssinia wanted to expand its lands and have more trading opportunities. The Abyssinians fought with Muslims in the area over who owned the coastlands—an important part of the trade routes. However, Abyssinia had better success with trade on the Blue Nile and over land.

Abyssinia used several techniques to get more land: religion, warfare, and diplomacy. It tended to target areas that were not Christian.

> **Interesting fact:** Most of the people around the Kingdom of Abyssinia were Muslim or still followed traditional African religions. There weren't a lot of other Christian countries in Africa at this time.

Abyssinian King Yagbea-Sion and his forces.
https://commons.wikimedia.org/wiki/File:YagbeaSionBattlingAdaSultan.JPG

The king encouraged people to move into newly-conquered territory by offering them pieces of land. This was called a **gult**. People who accepted land from the king could make the farmers on the land pay tribute, so it was a popular way for Abyssinia to maintain its hold on new lands.

One of the most famous Abyssinian rulers was **Amda Seyon I**. He ruled from 1314 to 1344 CE, and he is most famous for expanding Abyssinia.

Fasilides Palace.
Bernard Gagnon, CC BY-SA 3.0 <https://creativecommons.org/licenses/by-sa/3.0>,
via Wikimedia Commons; https://commons.wikimedia.org/wiki/File:Fasilides_Palace_02.jpg

Even though the Kingdom of Abyssinia wanted to expand its lands, many of its wars also focused on spreading Christianity. These were also **holy wars**. When **Zera Yakob** reigned in the 15th century, he defeated the Muslim countries on the coastlands.

Because Christianity was an important part of the kingdom, Abyssinia was also connected to Europe. During the Crusades, European countries tried to convince the Abyssinians to join them, but they did not help the Europeans in those holy wars.

Interesting fact: The Crusades were a series of wars the Europeans fought with the Muslims over the Holy Land. The Holy Land is in modern-day Israel and is an important place for Judaism, Christianity, and Islam.

Sadly, because it fought the Muslims throughout much of its history, the Kingdom of Abyssinia was no longer safe from the Muslim armies. The Muslim states banded together in the 1500s and attacked Abyssinia. They destroyed churches and even sacked **Axum**, one of the kingdom's major cities. The Kingdom of Abyssinia continued to weaken, but it had a revival in the mid-1800s.

COOL FACT: Ethiopia is one of two African countries that did not fall to colonialism. Colonialism is when a powerful country takes over a less powerful nation to take their resources. The Italians tried to take over Ethiopian land in 1896, but the Ethiopians pushed them back. They were able to keep their freedom and their country.

The Kingdom of Abyssinia finally ended in 1974 CE. Their last king was **Haile Selassie**. He wanted the government to become a **constitutional monarchy**, which would have given him a lot of power. However, the common people didn't think they had a voice in the government. When Haile Selassie did not try to help the people during famines in 1972 and 1974, they revolted and turned to **Marxist** ideas. In 1974, the Kingdom of Abyssinia fell, and **communism** took over the country.

The Kingdom of Abyssinia was an old kingdom. It saw many changes during its time in Africa and greatly impacted African culture. It reminds us that Africa developed many powerful civilizations during its history. Abyssinia had strong armies and a strong hold on its religion, impacting African history to this day.

Chapter 7 Activity

Can you answer the following questions in one to two sentences?

1. Who established the Kingdom of Abyssinia?

2. When was the kingdom established?

3. What other name is sometimes used to describe the Kingdom of Abyssinia?

4. Who was Yekuno Amlak?

5. What three techniques did the Kingdom of Abyssinia use to conquer land?

6. How long did the Kingdom of Abyssinia last?

Chapter 8: The Songhay Kingdom

The **Songhay Kingdom** was the last major pre-colonial kingdom in West Africa. At the height of its power, it stretched from the Atlantic Ocean to modern Niger. It ruled in West Africa from about 1464 to 1591 CE.

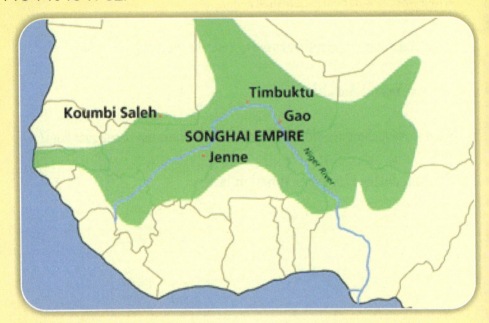

Songhay Empire map
No machine-readable author provided. Roke~commonswiki assumed (based on copyright claims)., CC BY-SA 3.0 <http://creativecommons.org/licenses/by-sa/3.0/>, via Wikimedia Commons https://commons.wikimedia.org/wiki/File:SONGHAI_empire_map.PNG

The Songhay people had actually been in the area since about 800 CE. They founded **Gao** as their capital, but it eventually became part of the Mali Empire. As the Mali Empire began to fade in the 1460s, the Songhay people rose up once again.

Fun Fact: The Songhay Kingdom never completely defeated the Mali Empire, but it soon became more powerful than Mali. The Mali Empire continued on the western edge of Songhay land until the 1600s.

Even though it had been part of the Mali Empire for many years, Songhay never really submitted to Mali's rule. The Songhay people controlled transportation on the Niger River, which made them powerful. In the 1400s, they began **raiding** Mali cities. Because of their constant fighting, the Songhay people finally won their freedom.

King Sunni Ali was the first Songhay ruler. He conquered cities like Timbuktu and gave his kingdom a strong start.

After King Sunni Ali died in 1492, his son took the throne, but he lost it after only one year to **Askia Muhammad Touré (Muhammed I).**

Interesting fact: Muhammad had to overthrow Sunni Ali's son to take the throne. His name was Sunni Baru.

Even though Muhammad I was a usurper, he still led the Songhay Kingdom during its golden age.

Fun Fact: "Askia" means "ruler" or "emperor."

Askia Muhammad I ruled from 1494 to 1528 CE. He expanded the empire even more, making the kingdom the largest it would ever be, and set up **provinces**. He set up the kingdom's first professional army and marched southeast, conquering land between the Niger River and Lake Chad.

Of course, Askia Muhammad was more than just a conqueror. He also invested in his kingdom. He made the government stronger by centralizing it.

COOL FACT: The king of Songhay was an absolute monarch, but there were many ministers and officials to help the king run the kingdom.

Muhammad was a Muslim, so he enforced Islamic laws and sent ambassadors to other Muslim states. He also built many schools throughout the kingdom and expanded Timbuktu's **University of Sankore**.

> **Interesting fact:** Even though Askia Muhammad was Muslim, Islam was mainly the religion of the upper class. Commoners, especially those living away from the cities, still practiced their traditional religion—an animist belief that certain things like trees and caves had spirits.

One of the main areas Askia Muhammad wanted the Songhay Kingdom to grow was trade. The Mali Empire had grown wealthy from trade because it had gold mines on its southern borders, but the Songhay Kingdom didn't have these.

In 1471, the **Portuguese** had sailed to West Africa and set up their own trading post. This trading post was another option that challenged the Trans-Saharan Trade Route. The Songhay Kingdom had to work hard to keep its resources and benefit from trade. They **monopolized** the Trans-Saharan Trade Route.

The Timbuktu Manuscripts.
https://commons.wikimedia.org/wiki/File:Timbuktu-manuscripts-astronomy-mathematics.jpg

Fun Fact: To monopolize something means someone has full control over creating or giving an item or service. How might a monopoly on the Trans-Saharan Trade Route have helped the Songhay Kingdom?

Timbuktu remained a thriving trade center. The Songhay Kingdom traded things like gold, spices, kola nuts, and enslaved people in exchange for salt, sugar, glass, and horses. Trade centers were not just markets. Instead, they were cities with schools, mosques, and houses built with stone. Most commoners lived on the city's outskirts in mud or reed houses, and farming remained an important part of their lives.

The Tomb of Askia in Gao.
Taguelmoust, CC BY-SA 3.0 <http://creativecommons.org/licenses/by-sa/3.0/>, via Wikimedia Commons; https://commons.wikimedia.org/wiki/File:Askia.jpg

When Askia Muhammad I died in 1528, he left behind a strong kingdom. It flourished for many years, and trade continued to support major cities like Timbuktu, Gao, and Djenné. Sadly, the Songhay Kingdom also had many civil wars after Muhammad died. People fought over the throne, and all of the wars weakened the kingdom. When another civil war erupted in 1591, **Sultan Ahmad I al-Mansur, a Saadi sultan,** decided to attack.

> **COOL FACT:** Sultan Ahmad I al-Mansur was the leader of Morocco. He wanted to control West Africa because he wanted the gold mines.

Askia Ishaq II was the last Songhay king, and he had an army with 30,000 soldiers and 10,000 cavalry riders. Ahmad I only sent 4,000 Moroccan soldiers to defeat the Songhay Kingdom, but they had new technology—muskets and cannons. The Songhay people were still fighting with arrows and spears, so the Moroccan army had the better weapons.

The Moroccans defeated the Songhay Kingdom and made it part of the Moroccan Empire. However, the Songhay people did not accept defeat quietly. They gave the Moroccans the same trouble they had given the Mali Empire. They rebelled and fought back, but it wasn't enough to save their kingdom. The Songhay Kingdom faded as the last of the powerful West African kingdoms.

The Songhay people were strong and determined to rule their own lives. They understood the importance of trade and believed in education and advancements. Although it no longer exists, the Songhay Kingdom shows how powerful the medieval African kingdoms were and the impact they made on the world.

Chapter 8 Activity

Can you decide which questions are true and which are false?

1. The Songhay Kingdom was founded by Emperor Mansa.

2. The Mali Empire ruled the Songhay Empire before Sunni Ali liberated it.

3. The empire reached its peak under the reign of Askia Muhammad.

4. The Moroccans invaded and conquered Gao and Timbuktu.

5. Askia Muhammad was a Christian and enforced Christianity during his reign.

6. The Moroccans beat the Songhay Kingdom because they had muskets and cannons.

7. The Songhay people were new to the area in 1461.

Chapter 9: Society and Famous Rulers

Medieval Africa had many famous rulers. They impacted their kingdoms' religion and daily lives and had a big impact on the world! Let's look at some of the most famous rulers from medieval Africa.

King Idris Alawma

King Idris Alawma was one of the greatest rulers of the **Kanem-Bornu Empire**. His reign started around 1564CE, but when he started his rule, Kanem and Bornu were separated. Bornu was ruling the empire by itself.

King Alawma wanted to expand his territory, so he made some changes to his military. He gave them new equipment like firearms, chainmail, and iron helmets. Idris Alawma also added musketeers, organized a new advanced guard and rear guard, and often used scorched earth policy to help his conquests. Alawma was an excellent military leader and reconquered Kanem. This re-solidified the Kanem-Bornu Empire.

However, political conquest was not his only focus. He also wanted to improve the government to better help the empire. He separated the **judiciary** branch from the rest of the government.

COOL FACT: The judiciary branch handles court cases and makes judgments when people break the law. What countries today separate their courts from other parts of the government?

Alawma also practiced Islam and encouraged his people to adopt the religion. He built new mosques and wanted people to make pilgrimages to Mecca. He worked hard with the Ottoman Empire to keep his people safe on their travels. The Kanem-Bornu Empire became more connected to the Muslim countries around them and did well under his rule.

Oba Ewuare the Great

Oba Ewuare the Great was one of the most famous rulers of the **Benin Empire**. He ruled from 1440 to 1473 CE and was remembered as a wise man. The oral stories say he was a great magician and warrior. While Ewuare led Benin, he added many new areas, including 201 new towns. He was certainly a good military leader!

Ewuare also focused on making the capital better. The capital city, called **Benin City**, received new roads and gateways while he ruled. Benin City was impressively organized. Oba Ewuare gave the city huge walls and a moat. The city was divided into districts. People grouped together in each district to practice their crafts and trades.

Oba Ewuare the Great.
Ebameful, CC BY-SA 4.0 <https://creativecommons.org/licenses/by-sa/4.0>, via Wikimedia Commons; https://commons.wikimedia.org/wiki/File:Oba_Ewuare_the_Great!.jpg

During his reign, Ewuare also encountered the **Portuguese**, sailing down the West African coast looking for new trade opportunities. Ewuare helped them build trade with the Benin Empire. This helped the empire grow economically. Under his rule, the empire prospered. Ewuare even encouraged people to make art, like wood and ivory carvings. Oba Ewuare the Great was one of the greatest Benin leaders and helped make the empire powerful.

Amda Seyon I

Amda Seyon I was one of the great leaders of the **Kingdom of Abyssinia**. He took the throne around 1314 CE and ruled until 1344 CE. He is most famous for doubling the size of the kingdom. Under his rule, Abyssinia reached from the Rift Valley to the Red Sea. Amda Seyon I also secured control over the central and southern parts of his kingdom, which had been less secure before.

COOL FACT: Amda Seyon I also dealt with succession issues by putting all of his male relations in a monastery except his sons. It kept the men from fighting civil wars for the throne. How would you feel about having to live in a monastery because you were related to the king?

Amda Seyon did not tolerate rebellions, and he treated the Muslim countries around him harshly. When lands under his power tried to break away, he killed anyone involved. Even though he was very harsh, Amda Seyon I created a strong kingdom that ruled the area for hundreds of years. He also encouraged trade. Historians believe the Kingdom of Abyssinia traded with the Byzantine Empire. They didn't only trade resources—they also exchanged books and written documents. Under Amda Seyon, Abyssinia's influence grew and changed the world.

An Ethiopian depiction of Amda Seyon I.

A. Davey from Where I Live Now: Pacific Northwest, CC BY 2.0 <https://creativecommons.org/licenses/by/2.0>, via Wikimedia Commons; https://commons.wikimedia.org/wiki/File:Ethiopian_Horses_(2427081498).jpg

Dawit II

Dawit II was a king of **Abyssinia** who ruled from around 1508 to 1540. His reign was very different than the rule of Amda Seyon. The Muslim forces had grown strong in the years since then, and they attacked starting in the 1520s. Dawit spent most of his reign fighting against them, but the Muslim armies gained ground.

Although Dawit II was not the last leader of Abyssinia, his rule was a dark time. There was a lot of fighting, and the Christian forces were struggling. He finally reached out to **Portugal** to ask for help, but they did not arrive until after he died in 1540. Thankfully, Abyssinia did not fall, but they were much smaller now. The kingdom would never be the same again.

Dawit II of Ethiopia, Emperor of Ethiopia.
https://commons.wikimedia.org/wiki/File:Cristofano_dell%E2%80%99Altissimo,_Portrait_of_Lebn%C3%A4-Dengel._c._1552-1568.jpg

Sunni Ali

Sunni Ali was the first king of the **Songhay Kingdom**—he began his rule around 1464. The Songhay Kingdom had just freed itself from the Mali Empire, which was falling apart. Sadly, they did not get a lot of land out of it. All they had was **Gao**, their capital.

COOL FACT: Gao was a strong trading center, but the Songhay Kingdom needed more than one city if they were going to survive.

Around 1468, Sunni Ali decided to put his military skills to use. He attacked cities like Mema, Djenné, and Timbuktu and captured them. He made sure his kingdom was connected to the Trans-Saharan Trade Route and defeated other tribes that would have attacked Songhay. This added new trading opportunities for the Songhay Kingdom, and the new lands brought wealth into the kingdom.

Sunni Ali was a talented military commander, but he was not always kind to the people he conquered. He was also known as **Sunni the Merciless**.

COOL FACT: **Ali's army had a special advantage over the cities it attacked. It had an armored cavalry and the only navy in North Africa."**

Although some of his methods were cruel, he is remembered today for giving his kingdom the foundation it needed to be strong for many years.

Askia Muhammad

Askia Muhammad ruled the **Songhay Kingdom** from 1494 to 1528 CE. He was a general under King Sunni Ali, but after he died around 1492, Muhammad decided to take the throne for himself.

Interesting fact: Muhammad had to overthrow Sunni Ali's son to take the throne. His name was **Sunni Baru**.

Muhammad was a good general but was even better at organizing a government. The new kingdom needed structure. He split the kingdom into **provinces** and set up a standing army. However, Muhammad was also a Muslim, so part of organizing the Songhay Kingdom included adding **Islamic laws**.

COOL FACT: **Many of the Islamic laws are found in the Koran.**

The Songhay Kingdom made **Arabic** its official written language, but it also made Islam the official religion for the nobility. Instead of encouraging people to adopt it, this made people leery of it. Still, the Songhay Kingdom became influential under Askia Muhammad, changing kingdoms beyond their borders.

Chapter 9 Activity

Can you match the rulers to their kingdoms? There might be more than one ruler per kingdom.

King Idris Alawma	The Songhay Kingdom
Askia Muhammad	The Kingdom of Abyssinia
Oba Ewuare the Great	The Kingdom of Benin
Amda Seyon I	The Kanem–Bornu Empire
Sunni Ali	Mali Empire
Dawit II	
Mansa Musa	

Chapter 10: Culture and Art

Medieval Africa was filled with many different kingdoms. They had great armies and were essential to global trade. Although they were powerful and changed the world, these kingdoms also produced beautiful art.

Some of this art came from the buildings they constructed. The Mali Empire built several mosques, and one of the most famous is the **Great Mosque of Djenné**.

Fun Fact: Djenné was an important city in the Mali Empire. It was part of the Trans-Saharan Trade Route and is one of the oldest cities in sub-Saharan Africa.

The Great Mosque at Djenné was built in the 1200s, but it was expanded multiple times. Because Mali could not access many stones, it was made from mud bricks and plaster. The building is a big rectangle, and it has a courtyard and a **prayer hall**. The prayer hall is so big that 3,000 people can fit inside! The mosque was built with traditional Mali architecture, with wooden beams sticking out of the walls to support the mud and plaster.

The Great Mosque of Djenné.
BluesyPete, CC BY-SA 3.0 <https://creativecommons.org/licenses/by-sa/3.0>,
via Wikimedia Commons; https://commons.wikimedia.org/wiki/File:MaliDjenn%C3%A9Mosqu%C3%A9e.JPG

Interesting fact: Buildings made of mud need more plaster every year to keep them in good shape. Can you imagine having to redo the walls of the Great Mosque in Djenné every year?

The Mali Empire also built the **Great Mosque of Timbuktu**. Timbuktu had many important buildings, especially when it became an important place for Muslim education. The Great Mosque in Timbuktu is one of three important mosques in the city.

Mansa Musa built the Great Mosque between 1325 and 1327, right after he returned from his pilgrimage to Mecca. This building has some, but most of it is built similarly to the Great Mosque in Djenné. The mud and wood buildings were traditional in Mali, but they required a lot of work to maintain!

Not all of the buildings constructed in Medieval Africa were mosques. In the Kingdom of Abyssinia, one of the most famous buildings is the **Church of Saint George** at Lalibela.

Fun Fact: Lalibela was an Ethiopian ruler, and he was so influential they renamed the city after him. One of his favorite activities was building churches.

According to legend, Lalibela had a vision. He was visited by an angel who told him how to build a church that would bring Heaven to Earth. Historians don't know if he really had a vision, but Lalibela immediately started building the Church of Saint George after that.

The church is special because it is carved out of volcanic rock. It's shaped like a cross and has many windows. The walls of the church stand over thirty yards high. That is over ninety feet tall! People had to carve tunnels to get to the church and then carve out the inside.

The inside of the church is beautiful. It is covered in **frescoes** about St. George and King Lalibela.

> **COOL FACT:** A fresco is a painting that is done in plaster. Frescos are usually painted onto walls and ceilings before the plaster can dry to make the paint permanent.

Church of Saint George.
Alastair Rae from London, United Kingdom, CC BY-SA 2.0
https://creativecommons.org/licenses/by-sa/2.0/; https://www.flickr.com/photos/merula/5343321137

These buildings show how beautiful architecture was during the Middle Ages in Africa. The people were imaginative and talented, but they didn't stop at buildings. They also made smaller pieces of art, like sculptures and pottery, and every empire had its own style. As you might remember, the Kingdom of Benin had special **brass plaques** in the palace filled with details about the king's life. They showed important leaders and warriors and decorated the pillars. Carving these scenes into the brass would have been difficult, but they did it without outside help.

Fun Fact: When the Europeans arrived in Benin, they were amazed by these brass plaques, just like we are today.

Of course, there were other kinds of art. Art also includes written documents. One of the most famous written texts from Medieval Africa comes from the Mali Empire, and it is called the **Timbuktu Manuscripts.**

Because Timbuktu was an academic center for hundreds of years, many people traveled from all over the world to learn. They didn't just learn about Islam. They also learned about biology, astronomy, math, and even music. Experts wrote down many things they were learning by hand and carefully saved them.

COOL FACT: The Timbuktu Manuscripts were written in medieval Arabic. Today, they have been translated into other languages, like English, Spanish, and modern Arabic.

A manuscript page from Timbuktu showing a table of astronomical information
https://commons.wikimedia.org/wiki/File:Timbuktu-manuscripts-astronomy-tables.jpg#/media/File:Timbuktu-manuscripts-astronomy-tables.jpg

There are over 40,000 pages in the Timbuktu Manuscripts, some of which were written in the 11th century. That was about a thousand years ago! Although some of the writing talks about **secular** topics, it also has early Qurans. It is an important national treasure for Mali, even though the empire has faded. The manuscripts remind the world that medieval Africa was a time filled with new discoveries as people explored the world around them and taught others about it.

Manuscript of Nasir al-Din Abu.
https://commons.wikimedia.org/wiki/File:Loc_timbuktu_manuscripts_amm0001rs.jpg

Medieval Africa was a vibrant time in African history. Many of the kingdoms and empires were heavily involved in trade. They changed the way people thought about travel and wealth. The people of Africa also adopted Islam into their culture, but they didn't get rid of their old beliefs and traditions. Instead, they merged new ideas with old ideas, creating something unique. Their leaders were strong warriors and government organizers, and their art reminds us that beauty is everywhere. We still have much to learn from medieval Africa, but it was an important part of how the world developed into what we know today.

Chapter 10 Activity

Can you pick which of the following monuments are from medieval Africa?

- St. Peter's Basilica

- Djinguereber Mosque

- Hagia Sophia

- Great Mosque of Djenné

- The Eiffel Tower

- Westminster Abbey

- Church of Saint George

Answer Key

Chapter : 1

Can you choose which of the achievements below came from the African Middle Ages?

- ~~Built the Great Wall of China~~
- <u>Developed a new language called Kiswahili</u>
- ~~Fought the Vikings~~
- <u>Built big trading cities and traded gold and salt</u>
- ~~Had famous jousting tournaments~~
- <u>Housed the Ghana and Mali Empires</u>
- <u>Adapted Islam to their traditions</u>
- ~~Were the first people to discover America.~~

Chapter : 2

1. The Ghana Empire was founded by King Soninke. False
2. The capital of the Kingdom of Ghana was Koumbi Saleh. True
3. The Soninke people were the enemies of the Ghana Empire. False
4. After its fall, the Ghana Empire became a part of the Kanem-Bornu Empire. False
5. The Ghana Empire made its wealth by trading items like gold and salt. True
6. Christians had their own part of the Ghana capital because they traded a lot with the empire. False
7. Ghana fell because they were invaded by the Roman Empire. False
8. The Ghana Empire was part of the Trans-Saharan Trade Route. True

Chapter : 3

2. The empire was founded by the Zaghawa and Kanembu nomadic people.
5. Dugu started the Duguwa dynasty.
3. The Kanem Empire expanded under Mai Dunama Dabbalemi.
4. Bornu recaptured its lost territories and became the Kanem-Bornu

Empire.
1. The reign of King Idris Alawma.
6. The Kanem-Bornu Empire ended and became the Borno Emirate.

Chapter : 4

1. What is another common name for the Kingdom of Benin?

    A) Kingdom of Ethiopia   B) Kingdom of Axum   **C) the Kingdom of Edo**

2. Who first established the Kingdom of Benin?

    A) Oba Ewuare the Great   **B) the Edo people**   C) King Solomon

3. What was the capital of the kingdom?

    A) Benin City   B) Ife   C) Timbuktu

4. Who conquered the Kingdom of Benin?

    A) The French   B) The Egyptians   **C) The British**

5. What kind of art is Benin most famous for?

    A) Paintings   **B) Brass plaques**   C) Stone sculptures

Chapter : 5

Can you match the king to his achievements? A king might have multiple achievements listed.

Mahmud IV   Sundiata Keita   Mansa Musa I

- United the tribes of the Malinke peoples and formed the Mali EmpireSundiata Keita
- Developed cities like Timbuktu and Gao into important cultural centers and improved the Mali EmpireMansa Musa I
- Was the last king of the Mali EmpireMahmud IV
- Name the Mali EmpireSundiata Keita
- Built Djinguereber, Timbuktu's Great MosqueMansa Musa I

Chapter : 6

2. Mansa Musa started his reign.
4. He revitalized and improved cities.

1. The pilgrimage to Mecca.
6. Sagmandia conquered Gao.
5. He built the Great Mosque at Timbuktu.
3. The *Catalan Atlas* was made with Musa on it.

Chapter : 7

1. Who established the Kingdom of Abyssinia?

   Yekuno Amlak started the Kingdom of Abyssinia.

2. When was the kingdom established?

   It was established in 1270 CE.

3. What other name is sometimes used to describe the Kingdom of Abyssinia?

   The Kingdom of Abyssinia is also called the Kingdom of Ethiopia.

4. Who was Yekuno Amlak?

   He was the first king of Abyssinia. He came from the Solomonid dynasty.

5. What three techniques did the Kingdom of Abyssinia use to conquer land?

   They used religion, warfare, and diplomacy.

6. How long did the Kingdom of Abyssinia last?

   The Kingdom of Abyssinia ended in 1974.

Chapter : 8

1. The Songhay Kingdom was founded by Emperor Mansa. **False**
2. The Songhay Kingdom was ruled by the Mali Empire before Sunni Ali liberated it. **True**
3. The empire reached its peak under the reign of Askia Muhammad. **True**
4. The Moroccans invaded and conquered Gao and Timbuktu. **True**
5. Askia Muhammad was a Christian and enforced Christianity during his reign. **False**

6. The Moroccans beat the Songhay Kingdom because they had muskets and cannons. **True**

7. The Songhay people were new to the area in 1461. **False**

Chapter : 9

King Idris Alawma— The Kanem–Bornu Empire

Askia Muhammad— Songhay Kingdom

Oba Ewuare the Great— The Kingdom of Benin

Amda Seyon I— The Kingdom of Abyssinia

Sunni Ali— Songhay Kingdom

Dawit II— The Kingdom of Abyssinia

Mansa Musa— Mali Empire

Chapter : 10

- ~~St. Peter's Basilica~~
- Djinguereber Mosque
- ~~Hagia Sophia~~
- Great Mosque of Djenné
- ~~The Eiffel Tower~~
- ~~Westminster Abbey~~
- Church of Saint George

If you want to learn more about tons of other exciting historical periods, check out our other books!

ANCIENT CIVILIZATIONS FOR KIDS

A CAPTIVATING GUIDE TO MESOPOTAMIA, EGYPT, THE EARLY CHINESE CIVILIZATION, THE MAYA, ANCIENT GREECE, AND ANCIENT ROME

CAPTIVATING HISTORY

Bibliography-African History for Kids

Want to know more about African history? Check out these books, websites, and videos!

Books:

Kanem-Borno: 1,000 Years of Splendor (The Kingdoms of Africa). Philip Koslow. 1995.

Black History: Kids Edition. Stephen Jones, Sr. 2015.

Who Was Nelson Mandela? Pam Pollack. 2014.

Websites:

https://www.ducksters.com/history/africa/ (Accessed November 2021)

https://www.rebekahgienapp.com/african-history/ (Accessed November 2021)

https://africa.mrdonn.org/ (Accessed November 2021)

Videos:

https://www.youtube.com/watch?v=AlnIdW0pu7o (Created December 2020)

https://www.youtube.com/watch?v=wqRXZJYeRzM (Created April 2016)

Bibliography-Ancient Africa for Kids

"Ancient Africa: Ancient Carthage." *Ducksters*. Accessed March 2022. https://www.ducksters.com/history/africa/ancient_carthage.php

"Ancient Africa: Empire of Ancient Ghana." *Ducksters*. Accessed March 2022. https://www.ducksters.com/history/africa/empire_of_ancient_ghana.php#:~:text=Ancient%20Ghana%20ruled%20from%20around,lands%20as%20they%20saw%20fit

"Ancient Africa: Kingdom of Aksum (Axum)." *Ducksters*. Accessed March 2022. https://www.ducksters.com/history/africa/kingdom_of_aksum_axum.php

"Ancient Africa: Kingdom of Kush (Nubia)." *Ducksters*. Accessed February 2022. https://www.ducksters.com/history/africa/kingdom_of_kush.php

"Ancient Egypt." *Britannica Kids*. Encyclopedia Britannica. Accessed February 2022. https://kids.britannica.com/kids/article/Ancient-Egypt/353087

"Ancient Egypt: Government." *Ducksters*. Accessed March 2022. https://www.ducksters.com/history/ancient_egyptian_government.php

"Ancient Egypt: Old Kingdom." *Ducksters*. Accessed February 2022. https://www.ducksters.com/history/ancient_egypt/old_kingdom.php

"Ancient Egypt: New Kingdom." *Ducksters*. Accessed February 2022. https://www.ducksters.com/history/ancient_egypt/new_kingdom.php

"Ancient Egypt: Pyramids." *Ducksters*. Accessed February 2022. https://www.ducksters.com/history/ancient_egyptian_pyramids.php

"Ancient Egypt: Timeline." *Ducksters*. Accessed February 2022. https://www.ducksters.com/history/ancient_egyptian_timeline.php

"Ancient Egyptian Alphabet." *History for Kids*. Accessed March 2022. https://www.historyforkids.net/ancient-egyptian-alphabet.html

"African Mythology." *Myths and Legends*. Accessed March 2022. http://www.mythencyclopedia.com/A-Am/African-Mythology.html

"Berbers." *Britannica Kids*. Encyclopedia Britannica. Accessed March 2022. https://kids.britannica.com/kids/article/Berbers/601928

"Biography: Hannibal Barca." *Ducksters*. Accessed March 2022. https://www.ducksters.com/history/africa/hannibal.php

Britannica, T. Editors of Encyclopedia. "Africa." *Encyclopedia Britannica*. March 29, 2018. https://www.britannica.com/place/Africa-Roman-territory

---. "Aksum." *Encyclopedia Britannica*. September 5, 2021. https://www.britannica.com/place/Aksum-ancient-kingdom-Africa

---. "Dogon." *Encyclopedia Britannica*. April 13, 2018. https://www.britannica.com/topic/Dogon

---. "Ghana." *Encyclopedia Britannica*. April 22, 2020. https://www.britannica.com/place/Ghana-historical-West-African-empire

---. "Piye." *Encyclopedia Britannica*, January 30, 2015. https://www.britannica.com/biography/Piye

Cartwright, Mark. "Kingdom of Axum." *World History Encyclopedia*. Last modified March 21, 2019. https://www.worldhistory.org/Kingdom_of_Axum

"Dogon." *Academic Kids Encyclopedia*. Accessed March 2022. https://academickids.com/encyclopedia/index.php/Dogon

Donn, Lin. "Ancient African Kingdom of Ghana." *Mr. Donn's Site for Kids & Teachers*. Accessed March 2022. https://africa.mrdonn.org/ghana.html

---. "Ancient Egypt for Kids: The Three Kingdoms." *Mr. Donn's Site for Kids & Teachers*. Accessed February 2022. https://egypt.mrdonn.org/3kingdoms.html

---. "Ancient Egypt for Kids: The Two Lands and King Menes." *Mr. Donn's Site for Kids & Teachers*. Accessed February 2022. https://egypt.mrdonn.org/twolands.html

---. "Ancient Kingdom of Kush (Nubia)." *Mr. Donn's Site for Kids & Teachers*. Accessed February 2022. https://africa.mrdonn.org/kush.html

---. "Hannibal and the Punic Wars." *Mr. Donn's Site for Kids & Teachers*. Accessed March 2022. https://rome.mrdonn.org/hannibal.html

"Egyptian Architecture." *History for Kids*. Accessed March 2022. https://www.historyforkids.net/ancient-egyptian-architecture.html

"Egyptian Art." *History for Kids*. Accessed March 2022. https://www.historyforkids.net/ancient-egyptia-art.html

"Egyptian Daily Life." *History for Kids*. Accessed March 2022. https://www.historyforkids.net/egyptian-daily-life.html

"Egyptian Pyramids." *History for Kids*. Accessed February 2022. https://www.historyforkids.net/egyptian-pyramids.html

"Egyptian Religion." *History for Kids*. Accessed March 2022. https://www.historyforkids.net/egyptian-religion.html

"Kingdom of Kerma: Facts for Kids." *Kiddle Encyclopedia*. November 2021. https://kids.kiddle.co/Kingdom_of_Kerma

"Kush." Encyclopedia Britannica. Accessed February 2022. https://kids.britannica.com/kids/article/Kush/353352

"Kushite Religion." Encyclopedia of Religion. *Encyclopedia.com*. February 28, 2022. https://www.encyclopedia.com/environment/encyclopedias-almanacs-transcripts-and-maps/kushite-religion

Mark, Joshua J. "Ancient Egyptian Mythology." *World History Encyclopedia*. Last modified January 17, 2013. https://www.worldhistory.org/Egyptian_Mythology

---. "Carthage." *World History Encyclopedia*. Last modified May 29, 2020. https://www.worldhistory.org/carthage

---. "The Kingdom of Kush." *World History Encyclopedia*. Last modified February 26, 2018. https://www.worldhistory.org/Kush

---. "Menes." *World History Encyclopedia*. Last modified January 29, 2016. https://www.worldhistory.org/Menes

"New Kingdom." *History for Kids*. Accessed February 2022. https://www.historyforkids.net/new-kingdom.html

New World Encyclopedia Contributors. "Berber." *New World Encyclopedia*. Accessed March 2022.
   https://www.newworldencyclopedia.org/p/index.php?title=Berber&oldid=1063295

---. "Ghana Empire." New World Encyclopedia. Accessed March 2022.

https://www.newworldencyclopedia.org/p/index.php?title=Ghana_Empire&oldid=1005238

"Old Kingdom." *History for Kids*. Accessed February 2022. https://www.historyforkids.net/old-kingdom.html

"Religion of Ancient Egypt: Facts of Kids." *Kiddle Encyclopedia*. Last modified July 16, 2021. https://kids.kiddle.co/Religion_of_Ancient_Egypt

"Roman Africa." *Oxford Reference*. Accessed March 2022. https://www.oxfordreference.com/view/10.1093/oi/authority.20110803095354714

Sue, Caryl. "The Kingdom of Kush." *National Geographic Society*. July 2018. https://www.nationalgeographic.org/media/kingdoms-kush

"The Archaic Period." *History for Kids*. Accessed February 2022. https://www.historyforkids.net/the-archaic-period.html

"The Great Sphinx." *History for Kids*. Accessed February 2022. https://www.historyforkids.net/the-great-sphinx.html

"The Kingdom of Kerma (2500-1500 BC)." *Think Africa*. November 2018. https://thinkafrica.net/the-kingdom-of-kerma-2500-1500-bc

Bibliography-Medieval Africa for Kids

"Ancient Africa for Kids: Empire of Ancient Ghana." Ducksters. Technological Solutions, Inc. (TSI). Accessed April 2023. https://www.ducksters.com/history/africa/empire_of_ancient_ghana.php.

"Ancient Africa for Kids: Empire of Ancient Mali." Ducksters. Technological Solutions, Inc. (TSI). Accessed April 2023. https://www.ducksters.com/history/africa/empire_of_ancient_mali.php.

"Amda Seyon." *EthiopianHistory*.com. Accessed April 2023. https://ethiopianhistory.com/Amda_Seyon/.

"Amda Seyon I Facts for Kids." *Kiddle Encyclopedia*. February 2023. https://kids.kiddle.co/Amda_Seyon_I.

"Bornu Empire." *Lumen Learning*. Accessed April 2023. https://courses.lumenlearning.com/suny-hccc-worldcivilization/chapter/bornu-empire/.

Britannica, T. Editors of Encyclopedia. "Benin." *Encyclopedia Britannica*. March 2023. https://www.britannica.com/place/Benin-historical-kingdom-West-Africa.

---. "Ghana." *Encyclopedia Britannica*. March 2023.

https://www.britannica.com/place/Ghana-historical-West-African-empire.

---. "Kanem-Bornu." *Encyclopedia Britannica*. April 2023. https://www.britannica.com/place/Kanem-Bornu.

---. "Mali." *Encyclopedia Britannica*. April 2023. https://www.britannica.com/place/Mali-historical-empire-Africa.

---. "Songhai Empire." *Encyclopedia Britannica*. April 2023. https://www.britannica.com/place/Songhai-empire.

---. "Sonni ʿAlī." *Encyclopedia Britannica*. January 2023. https://www.britannica.com/biography/Sonni-Ali.

Cartwright, Mark. "Ghana Empire." *World History Encyclopedia*. UNESCO Archives. March 2019. https://www.worldhistory.org/Ghana_Empire/.

---. "Kingdom of Abyssinia." *World History Encyclopedia*. UNESCO Archives. April 2019. https://www.worldhistory.org/Kingdom_of_Abyssinia/.

---. "Kingdom of Benin." *World History Encyclopedia*. UNESCO Archives. April 2019. https://www.worldhistory.org/Kingdom_of_Benin/.

---. "Kingdom of Kanem." *World History Encyclopedia*. UNESCO Archives. April 2019. https://www.worldhistory.org/Kingdom_of_Kanem/.

---. "Mali Empire." *World History Encyclopedia*. UNESCO Archives. March 2019. https://www.worldhistory.org/Mali_Empire/.

---. "Mansa Musa I." *World History Encyclopedia*. UNESCO Archives. February 2019. https://www.worldhistory.org/Mansa_Musa_I/.

---. "Songhai Empire." *World History Encyclopedia*. UNESCO Archives. March 2019. https://www.worldhistory.org/Mansa_Musa_I/.

---. "The Spread of Islam in Ancient Africa." *World History Encyclopedia*. UNESCO Archives. May 2019. https://www.worldhistory.org/article/1382/the-spread-of-islam-in-ancient-africa/.

"Church of Saint George." *Brilliant Ethiopia*. Accessed April 2023. https://www.brilliant-ethiopia.com/church-of-saint-george.

"Dawit II." *Wikipedia*. April 2023. https://en.wikipedia.org/wiki/Dawit_II.

Department of the Arts of Africa, Oceania, and the Americas. "Trade and the Spread of Islam in Africa." *Heilbrunn Timeline of Art History*. New York: The Metropolitan Museum of Art. October 2001. http://www.metmuseum.org/toah/hd/tsis/hd_tsis.htm.

Donn, Lin. "Ancient African Kingdom of Ghana." *Mr. Donn's Site for Kids and Teachers*. Accessed April 2023. https://africa.mrdonn.org/ghana.html

"Ethiopian Empire." *New World Encyclopedia*. Accessed April 2023. https://www.newworldencyclopedia.org/entry/Ethiopian_Empire.

Fauvelle, François-Xavier. "Africa's Medieval Golden Age." *History Extra*.

Immediate Media Company Limited. July 2020. https://www.historyextra.com/period/what-was-africa-like-middle-ages-medieval-golden-age-culture/.

Foster, Clint. "Africa in the Middle Ages: What Was Medieval African Culture?" *Study.com*. Accessed March 2023. https://study.com/learn/lesson/medieval-africa-history-culture-people.html#:~:text=The%20medieval%20period%20in%20Africa,500%20CE%20to%201500%20CE.

"Ghana Empire Facts for Kids." *Kiddle Encyclopedia*. July 2022. https://kids.kiddle.co/Ghana_Empire.

Graft-Johnson, J. Coleman de. "Mūsā I of Mali." *Encyclopedia Britannica*. October 2022. https://www.britannica.com/biography/Musa-I-of-Mali.

"Idris Alawma." *Encyclopedia Britannica*. Accessed April 2023. https://www.britannica.com/biography/Idris-Alawma.

"Kanem–Bornu Empire Facts for Kids." *Kiddle Encyclopedia*. March 2023. https://kids.kiddle.co/Kanem%E2%80%93Bornu_Empire.

"Mai Idris Alooma." World Eras. *Encyclopedia.com*. April 2023. https://www.encyclopedia.com/history/news-wires-white-papers-and-books/mai-idris-alooma.

"Mali Empire Facts for Kids." Kiddle Encyclopedia. August 2022. https://kids.kiddle.co/Mali_Empire.

"Mansa Musa Facts for Kids." Kiddle Encyclopedia. April 2023. https://kids.kiddle.co/Mansa_Musa.

Maseko, Nomsa. "Timbuktu Manuscripts: Mali's Ancient Documents Captured Online." *BBC*. March 2022. https://www.bbc.com/news/world-africa-60689699.

MasterClass. "Great Mosque of Djenné: History and Architecture of the Djenné Mosque." *MasterClass*. September 2021. https://www.masterclass.com/articles/great-mosque-of-djenne.

"Medieval Africa." *World History with Mrs. Bailey*. Accessed March 2023. https://whbailey.weebly.com/africa-in-the-middle-ages.html.

"Oba Ewuare Ogidigan." World Eras. *Encyclopedia.com*. April 2023. https://www.encyclopedia.com/history/news-wires-white-papers-and-books/oba-ewuare-ogidigan.

Rouch, J. Pierre. "Muḥammad I Askia." *Encyclopedia Britannica*. February 2023. https://www.britannica.com/biography/Muhammad-I-Askia.

Tesfu, Julianna. "Songhai Empire (ca. 1375-1591)." *BlackPast.org*. June 2008. https://www.blackpast.org/global-african-history/songhai-empire-ca-1375-1591/#:~:text=The%20Songhai%20Empire%20was%20the,Northwest%20Nigeria

%20and%20central%20Niger.

The British Museum. "The Kingdom of Benin." *Smarthistory*.

"The Djinguereber Mosque." *Abdullatif Al Fozan Award for Mosque Architecture*. Accessed April 2023. https://mosqpedia.org/en/mosque/1101.

"The Expansion of Islam and Trade in Africa." *PBS*. PBS & GBH Educational Foundation. Accessed March 2023. https://myarkansaspbs.pbslearningmedia.org/resource/a12a7d79-ca45-42db-8299-f009a9f3d0a0/the-expansion-of-islam-and-trade-in-africa/.

"The Kingdom of Benin." *National Geographic*. May 2022. https://education.nationalgeographic.org/resource/kingdom-benin/.

Made in the USA
Coppell, TX
18 September 2023